# ENGAGE

## THE

# F  X

# ENGAGE

## THE

# FX

JEN LAWRENCE &
LARRY CHESTER

GREENLEAF
BOOK GROUP PRESS

Published by Greenleaf Book Group Press
Austin, Texas
www.gbgpress.com

Distributed by Greenleaf Book Group

For ordering information or special discounts for bulk purchases, please contact Greenleaf Book Group at PO Box 91869, Austin, TX 78709, 512.891.6100.

Design and composition by Greenleaf Book Group
Cover design by Greenleaf Book Group

Cataloging-in-Publication data
Lawrence, Jen, 1972-
    Engage the fox : a business fable about thinking critically and motivating your team / Jen Lawrence & Larry Chester.—First edition.
        pages : illustrations ; cm
    Based on Larry Chester's popular course in critical thinking.
    Variants of authors' names appear on cover image.
    Subtitle from cover.
    Issued also as an ebook.
    Includes bibliographical references and index.
    1. Decision making.  2. Critical thinking.  3. Employee motivation.
4. Organizational change.  I. Chester, Larry.  II. Title.

HD30.23 .L39 2014
658.4/03                                          2014936875


ISBN 13: 978-1-62634-123-4

Part of the Tree Neutral® program, which offsets the number of trees consumed in the production and printing of this book by taking proactive steps, such as planting trees in direct proportion to the number of trees used: www.treeneutral.com

TreeNeutral®

Printed in the United States of America on acid-free paper

14 15 16 17 18 19   10 9 8 7 6 5 4 3 2 1

First Edition

*To India and Archie*

# CONTENTS

# INTRODUCTION

For the past twenty-five years, I have trained thousands of professionals to manage projects, manage people, and think more strategically on the job. For years, my clients have been telling me that I ought to write a book so that the processes I've developed can be shared with those who are not able to attend one of my corporate or university training sessions. First, I wanted to write a book based on Process Design Consultants Inc.'s Critical Thinking program, which teaches participants how to recognize and resolve problems and maximize opportunities.

The Critical Thinking program was born out of the idea that, in spite of all of our knowledge of management theory, 60-70 percent of business projects do not achieve the desired results. Furthermore, of that 60-70 percent, an estimated 20 percent of business projects fail entirely. By teaching our clients a simple thinking process to identify the cause of problems, generate solutions, evaluate options, and ensure buy-in, we have increased their success rate. The classes we run are very interactive, and participants work on business issues they are facing on a real-time basis. We incorporate a discussion of the Myers-Briggs Type Indicator (MBTI®) in our sessions and use the MBTI® assessment tool to help our corporate clients better understand their personal thinking styles. The challenge was trying to capture all of this in book form.

My coauthor and colleague, Jen Lawrence, thought that a fable about a fictional company facing some major problems was the best way to take the reader through the thinking process. We decided to concoct a regional newspaper, *The Toad Hollow Gazette*, as our setting, since traditional media companies are facing a period of intense change. Although Jen and I have both worked with clients in the newspaper industry, the setting, characters, and plot are complete works of the imagination. We needed to create a memorable management team for our newspaper and thought that animals, with their unique characteristics, work well as archetypes representing facets of the thinking process. For years, I've used the expression "Engage the Fox" to describe how companies undergoing a strategic shift need to involve people who are adept at navigating change. There is also an expression used in management and political theory that is attributed to 7th century BCE poet, Archilochus: "The fox knows many things; the hedgehog one big thing." We thought it would be fun to have a hedgehog as the publisher and CEO who has lived and breathed newspapers for his entire career. His counterpoint is the consultant fox who "knows many things" and brings in that outsider perspective. We rounded out the management team with some key players who exemplify the four-step critical thinking process:

## Critical Thinking Process

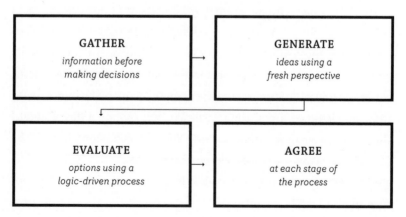

In order to think your way through a problem, you first need to *gather* as much information as you can so you can begin to figure out the problem's root cause. We thought that a squirrel represented a capable gatherer and made him the newspaper's head of advertising sales. After you know what is causing the problem, you need to start to *generate* some solutions. Our consultant fox is up to this task since, as an outsider, he offers a fresh perspective. Once you have all of the possible solutions on the table, you need to devise a way to methodically *evaluate* the options. Owls are known for their wisdom and their ability to sit up high and analyze the situation, so we made an owl the newspaper's finance director. Finally, we needed someone to make sure that all of the key stakeholders *agree* with the decision and have buy-in. Human Resources often takes on this role in a company, so we made a dog, a known social animal, head of Animal Resources (or, as our forest creatures call it, AR.)

Just in case you are worried that a fox, dog, owl, hedgehog, and squirrel might not get along very well, the animals have signed a peace treaty doing away with the concept of predators and prey. We promise you that no animals were harmed in the making of this book.

As the creatures of *The Toad Hollow Gazette* resolve the issues they face, you will become well-versed in the four-step critical thinking process that can help you approach any issue you might have to face: from how to deal with a shift in the competitive environment to what to have for supper tonight. You will also learn the four key critical thinking skills that can help you manage complex, messy issues in a systematic way that elicits stakeholder buy-in and maximizes success. You will note that each of the four critical thinking skills uses the four steps of the basic critical thinking process.

## Critical Thinking Skills for Issues Management

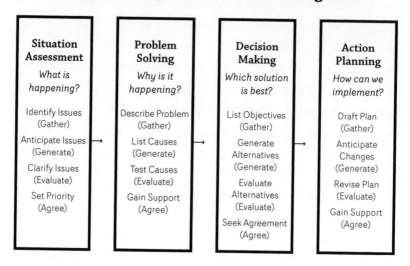

| Situation Assessment | Problem Solving | Decision Making | Action Planning |
|---|---|---|---|
| *What is happening?* | *Why is it happening?* | *Which solution is best?* | *How can we implement?* |
| Identify Issues (Gather) | Describe Problem (Gather) | List Objectives (Gather) | Draft Plan (Gather) |
| Anticipate Issues (Generate) | List Causes (Generate) | Generate Alternatives (Generate) | Anticipate Changes (Generate) |
| Clarify Issues (Evaluate) | Test Causes (Evaluate) | Evaluate Alternatives (Evaluate) | Revise Plan (Evaluate) |
| Set Priority (Agree) | Gain Support (Agree) | Seek Agreement (Agree) | Gain Support (Agree) |

By the time you reach the end of this book, you should be as well-versed in critical thinking as our characters are.

Happy reading, and, as Fox likes to say, *May the process be with you.*

Larry Chester

Process Design Consultants Inc.

# CAST OF CHARACTERS

## TOAD HOLLOW GAZETTE EXECUTIVE TEAM:
Toad Sr.—*Chair of the Board*
Hedgehog—*Publisher*
Squirrel—*Advertising Director*
Owl—*Finance Director*
Dog—*Animal Resources Director*
Fieldmouse—*Executive Assistant to Hedgehog*
Rabbit—*Editor in Chief*
Deer—*Circulation Director*
Badger—*Production Director*
Coyote—*Information Technology Director*
Toad Jr.—*Promotions Director*

## ASSOCIATES:
Thaddeus P. Fox—*Consultant*
Rat—*Banker*
Beaver—*Recruiter*

## MAJOR CLIENTS:
Raccoon Auto Mart
Big Bear Real Estate
Turtle Travel
Magpie Jewelers

# CHAPTER ONE

# TROUBLE AT *THE TOAD HOLLOW GAZETTE*

Things were grim at *The Toad Hollow Gazette*.

Raccoon had threatened to pull her business if the paper did not give her a 15 percent discount on all future Raccoon Auto Mart advertisements. Raccoon was the newspaper's largest client and they could not afford to lose her business.

Fieldmouse poked his head into Hedgehog's office. "I have Toad Sr. on the line for you," he said.

Hedgehog sighed. Toad Sr. was the chair of the board and Hedgehog's boss. Hedgehog had been hoping to delay telling Toad Sr. about the problem until he had a solution to propose. His head of ad sales was pulling together some information about Raccoon's account.

"Tell him I'm in a meeting," Hedgehog said.

"I don't think that's a good idea," said Fieldmouse. "He said he needed to talk to you immediately about advertising."

Hedgehog sighed. Raccoon must have contacted Toad Sr. directly.

"How did he sound?" Hedgehog asked.

"Angry," Fieldmouse stated. "He kept calling me Rodent."

"I'm sorry," said Hedgehog. "Put the call through."

Hedgehog took a deep breath and pressed the flashing button on his speaker phone. "Sorry to keep you waiting, Toad," he said.

"Hedgehog!" the newspaper's Chair of the Board barked. Hedgehog could practically smell the cigar smoke over the phone line. "I just had a perfectly fine golf game ruined when I was interrupted on the 16th hole by our clients demanding discounts. What in tarnation is going on?"

"I'm so sorry," Hedgehog started to explain. "I was about to call you. Raccoon has threatened to pull all of her ad business unless we offer her a 15 percent discount."

"Raccoon?" Toad Sr. interrupted. "I'm talking about Bear, Turtle, and Magpie. They told me that you are offering everybody a discount. I had no idea what they were talking about, and looked like an idiot."

Raccoon, Bear, Turtle, and Magpie were Toad's golfing buddies. Together, they were the four largest advertisers at *The Gazette*.

"I'm sorry," Hedgehog stammered. "Raccoon just called us yesterday."

"You need to let me know these things right away. I'll remind you that I'm the owner of this newspaper. And your boss." Toad Sr. snapped.

How could he forget that? During the interview process, Hedgehog had been led to believe that, as the new publisher of *The Gazette*, he would be fully in charge. But it had been hard for Toad Sr. to relinquish control after running the paper for most of his life. Hedgehog understood that as the first non-family CEO in the paper's history he'd have to work to build trust, but he had risked a lot to take this job, leaving his job as editor in chief of *The Meadowvale Tribune* and relocating his wife and hoglets to Toad Hollow. Plus, he'd just taken out a considerable mortgage on his new home in Toad Hollow and would likely lose a lot of money if this job did not work out. The lack of support from Toad Sr. made him very nervous.

"We can't afford to give a 15 percent discount," said Hedgehog. "Margins are thin enough as it is."

"These guys made it pretty clear that they will pull their business if you don't extend them discounts," Toad Sr. replied.

"I'll meet with Squirrel and Owl and we will brainstorm some solutions," Hedgehog said, trying to sound positive.

"These had better be some pretty darn good solutions," said Toad Sr. "Since you've come on board, readership is down, ad revenues are down, and we keep losing business to the Internet. I've had this paper in my family for over a hundred years and I won't let it bleed to death on your watch. I'd rather shut it down."

"I've promised to get back to Raccoon and the major advertisers by Friday. The others will have to wait until Friday too," said Hedgehog. "I'll let you know what we are thinking as soon as I meet with my team."

"Then you'd better get to work!" Toad Sr. snapped. "If you can't find a solution by Friday, I'm going to shut down the paper. Toad Jr. made some pretty good money doing startups and I'd be better off investing my money with him." Hedgehog heard a sharp click and then a dial tone. Toad Sr. had hung up on him.

Hedgehog put his head in his paws and took a deep breath. He was annoyed that Toad Sr. was trying to blame the long-standing problems of the paper on him. Part of the reason the board wanted an outsider is that things had been slipping for years. Toad Jr. might be the apple of his father's eye, but the board viewed him as a flaky dilettante. The newspaper business in general was going through hard times, and Toad Hollow had been harder hit by the depressed economy than many other areas in the forest. Hedgehog had been hired for his proven newspaper expertise and had been promised the resources to help turn the paper around: resources that had yet to materialize. He really wished that he had a mentor with whom to discuss things, as he'd had earlier in his career.

Hedgehog took another deep breath and picked up the phone. "Squirrel, can you come into my office now? Bring all of the data you have about our top ten accounts. And bring Owl. I want to see how any changes to our ad contracts will impact our finances."

"What's going on?" Owl asked when she arrived at Hedgehog's

office with Squirrel. As finance director, she was seldom brought into emergency meetings to discuss *good* news.

"It's the advertisers," Hedgehog explained. "Raccoon is demanding a 15 percent discount in order to continue with her advertising contract. Now it looks like Big Bear Real Estate, Turtle Travel, and Magpie Jewelers are going to push for discounts too."

"We cannot give our top four advertisers a 15 percent discount," said Owl. "Margins are tight enough as it is. I was talking to our banker today and he said that we are getting close to breaking the terms of our banking agreement. If we lose their ad business, the bank will pull our operating lines."

"You called the bank?" Hedgehog asked.

"They called me," Owl said. "Our last quarter was weak and they are pretty concerned. Some other newspapers have gone out of business and their bankers have taken a hit. If we lose our top four advertisers, they won't be happy. Do you really think Raccoon and the others will walk? Perhaps it's just an idle threat."

"Raccoon just pulled all of her billboard advertising because the outdoor media company would not negotiate," Squirrel said. "She took that business online."

"Can she just walk away from contracts like that?" Owl asked.

Squirrel nodded. "She's been in touch with her lawyer. He told her that our readership numbers have dropped and we may have breached the performance clause in the contract. It looks like she and the others have an out."

"So, it sounds like we need to offer the discount," Hedgehog sighed. He had no idea that some advertisers were exiting certain media. He'd assumed it was simply a threat to negotiate better terms. "But we cannot lose any revenue."

"We can always offer the discount and cut expenses by 15 percent to offset the decrease in revenue," Owl said. "Our bankers would be fine with that."

"Reduce head count?" Squirrel asked nervously.

"We'd pretty much have to. Employee salaries are the bulk of our cost base and newsprint and ink prices are what they are." Hedgehog said glumly.

"Or we could increase other revenue," Squirrel offered.

"We aren't going to solve it tonight," Hedgehog said. "Squirrel, can you leave me the information you pulled about the advertisers? Owl, can you do up a spreadsheet by tomorrow that shows what our financial projections look like with the requested ad discount?"

Both animals nodded and headed back to their offices. Hedgehog told his assistant, Fieldmouse, to go home. He did not think he needed to tell the others about Toad Sr.'s threat to shut down the paper. He hoped it was a scare tactic. And even if it wasn't, there was no point in panicking the others.

Hedgehog pored over spreadsheets and looked at publicly available information about what other papers were doing. By the time Hedgehog finally turned off his computer, it was after 9:00 p.m.

Hedgehog's wife, Cindy, and the hoglets were visiting Cindy's parents for the week. Hedgehog could not face going home to an empty house and decided to have a decaf coffee and a slice of pecan pie at the Smiling Moose Café. He parked his car in front of the home he and his family had bought just over a year ago and walked to Main Street, where there were a few shops and restaurants. Some stores were papered over with faded For Lease signs hanging in the windows. Toad Hollow had been hit hard when Glenwide, the discount mortgage company that had employed much of the town, went bankrupt several years before. *The Gazette* had experienced a huge decline in readers as animals left town permanently to try to find work.

The Smiling Moose Café was packed. A flyer on the door indicated that it was Poetry Slam night. Fieldmouse was on the stage wearing a black beret, cradling a set of bongo drums. In spite of his curiosity about the poetry talents of his assistant, Hedgehog had no desire to hang out with creatures from work. Just as he had resigned himself to eating leftover takeout and watching TV, he noticed the neon red "Open" sign in the window of the Tipsy Marmot Tavern across the street. He'd never been much of a bar guy, but the thought of going home and watching D-list celebrities attempting to ballroom dance was depressing. He pushed open the heavy door.

A wild boar stood polishing glasses behind the old-fashioned wood and brass bar. The tables were all taken, so Hedgehog walked over to the bar and took a seat on one of the tall wooden stools.

"A sidecar, please," he said to the boar.

The boar raised an eyebrow but pulled a bottle of cognac from the shelf.

"You're not a regular here, are you?" said a smooth voice.

Hedgehog looked up. He'd been so focused on his work problems that he'd not even noticed the fox sitting one seat over. He was well dressed and looked as though he belonged in a Creeks Brothers catalog. Hedgehog guessed he was from out of town.

"I'm not really a bar guy," Hedgehog confessed.

"Tough day?" the fox asked.

"You could say that," Hedgehog said, hoping that this fox character would get the hint that he was not in a talking mood.

"Creatures tell me I'm a good listener," said the fox, holding out his paw to shake. "Thaddeus P. Fox."

Hedgehog extended his paw somewhat reluctantly. In spite of the peace treaty, he was always a bit nervous around foxes. His grandfather had been eaten by one.

The wild boar slid the drink across the bar toward Hedgehog.

"Cheers," said Fox, raising his glass.

"Cheers," said Hedgehog. He took a sip of his drink.

The two sat in silence, watching the bartender stack glasses.

Cindy was always telling Hedgehog that he had to be friendlier and make more of an effort with strangers. He decided to engage the fox in conversation. If nothing else, it might take his mind off work.

"So, are you drowning your sorrows too?" Hedgehog asked.

"Me?" asked Fox. "No. I'm in town on business and I'd rather be out with creatures than sitting in some hotel room watching cable."

"Me too. My wife and kids are out of town, work was awful, and I'm here avoiding that celebrity dancing show on TV," Hedgehog confessed.

Fox chuckled. "That show is the worst. My mother loves it. Whenever I phone her to see how she's doing, it seems to be on."

Hedgehog laughed. "What line of work are you in?" he asked.

"I'm a corporate consultant," said Fox. "I help companies solve problems."

"I know about management consultants," Hedgehog said. He was not used to drinking and the sidecar was encouraging him to speak freely. "We hired a bunch of you guys when I worked for *The Meadowvale Tribune* in their management training program. A bunch of 25-year-olds fresh out of biz school showed up, gave us a bunch of suggestions that didn't really apply to our business, and charged us a fortune for the privilege."

Fox smiled. "There are a lot of ineffective consultants out there," he said.

"Want to hear a joke?" asked Hedgehog.

"Sure," said Fox.

"Okay," Hedgehog started. "How many consultants does it take to change a light bulb?"

"I don't know: How many consultants does it take to change a light bulb?" Fox asked, playing along.

"It depends," Hedgehog deadpanned. "How large is your budget?"

Fox laughed. "That's a good one."

"So, what exactly is it that you do, consulting-wise?" Hedgehog asked.

"I teach critical thinking," Fox stated.

"So, you are in town to teach someone how to think?" Hedgehog asked. "Because I already know how to do that."

Fox smiled. "Most creatures think that they know how to think."

"Are you saying that they don't?" asked Hedgehog.

"When your wife was pregnant with your first hoglet, did you attend any prenatal classes?" Fox asked.

"Of course," Hedgehog said.

"What did they focus on?" Fox asked.

"Um, I can't really remember. It was a while ago. They told me I had to run for ice chips and Cindy had to learn how to breathe." Hedgehog said.

"Did your wife not know how to breathe before she was pregnant?" Fox asked.

"Okay, I see your point. But they were teaching her how to breathe through labor." Hedgehog said.

"And do you know why they did that?" Fox asked.

"Well, they said that a lot of creatures panic when they are in labor and forget to breathe. It's a new situation and you are in a lot of pain. You can pass out if you forget to breathe," Hedgehog explained.

"It's kind of the same way with thinking," Fox said. "When we are panicked, we often forget how to think. We make assumptions, we jump the gun, or we freeze. I have a framework to help clients think clearly about issues even when they are in stressful situations."

"Does it work?" Hedgehog asked.

"I've coached thousands of professionals over the years," Fox said. "They tell me it works."

Hedgehog paused. He had a lot of decisions to make these days. This was the kind of help he needed. "Do you have a business card?" he asked.

Fox handed him a business card: simple heavy white cardstock with "Thaddeus P. Fox" and a phone number in black ink. On the back was a two-by-two matrix:

## Critical Thinking Process

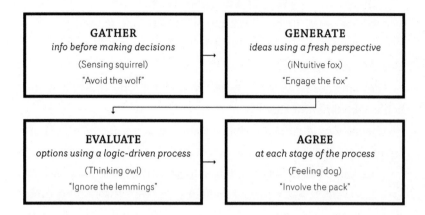

"Is this your thinking process?" Hedgehog asked.

"It is," Fox nodded.

"Ever do any work in the newspaper business?" Hedgehog asked.

"I've worked with media companies," Fox said. "But I've never done work for a newspaper."

"That's too bad," Hedgehog said. "I could use someone like you, but I need someone who understands my business."

"The less I know about your business, the fewer biases I bring into the room," Fox said. "My job is to help companies develop an effective framework for thinking. Much of what I do involves asking good questions. It's hard to ask good questions when your head is already filled with answers."

"Fox," Hedgehog said, "I need to level with you. I've had a horrible day at work. For some reason I like you and think that in other circumstances you could help me . . . "

"I hear a 'but'," Fox said.

"But I need someone who understands the newspaper business. We are not like other businesses. I need to hire one of those consulting firms with a large media group," Hedgehog said.

"They will tell you how you can be a better newspaper," Fox said.

"Exactly," Hedgehog said.

"Do you even want to be a newspaper?" Fox said.

"Do we want to be a newspaper?" Hedgehog gasped incredulously. "What else could we be? Oh, don't tell me. We should be a blog. Or a Facebook page."

Fox shrugged, "As I said, I don't know. Only you and your stakeholders would know that."

Hedgehog sighed. Consultants were so frustrating. So often they talked in riddles.

Fox looked at his watch. "Sorry to call it a night, but I have an early morning. It was a pleasure meeting you. There is just one thing that I want to leave with you. You've mentioned several times tonight that you have to make this decision all on your own. I promise you that you don't and you shouldn't. Involve the pack. And if you ever want my help, please give me a call. I'd be happy to talk to you more about my methodology."

He shook Hedgehog's paw and left the bar.

Hedgehog figured he should call it a night too. He asked the bartender to give him the bill.

"Your friend took care of it," Boar said. "Good tipper, too."

Hedgehog had not even seen Fox pay.

He put on his coat and did up the buttons even though he was only a couple of blocks from his house. The air had turned chilly over the past couple of weeks. He could sense winter was coming. Part of him wished he could simply hibernate so he would not have to deal with this situation at work.

That night, as he lay in his bed, trying to fall asleep, he thought about what Fox had said. Did *The Gazette* want to be a newspaper? Was that actually a choice? Fox had also urged him not to make the decision on his own. They all acted like lone wolves at the paper these days. Hedgehog felt he had to solve the advertising problem before involving Toad. Owl had been talking to the banker without letting

Hedgehog know. Maybe he needed to get everyone in a room to solve this advertising problem.

He typed out a quick e-mail to the full management team, telling them that he wanted them in a 10:00 a.m. meeting to discuss options around the advertisers' demands. He hoped that someone might have some ideas they could use.

# CHAPTER TWO

# DISSIDENCE AMONG THE RANKS

Hedgehog walked into the boardroom at exactly 10:00 a.m. Field-mouse was there to take notes. Hedgehog hoped that he had not stayed up too late reading poetry and playing the bongos at the coffee house.

Hedgehog cleared his throat. "Thanks for making time for this meeting on such short notice," he said. "The reason I called you here is that, as you are all aware, our business has been going through tough times. Our readership numbers have not been growing and our advertisers can reach more viewers for far less money online. Our top four advertisers are demanding significant discounts and we cannot afford to lose any more revenue without an equal offset in costs. We need to come up with a solution by the end of business tomorrow to present to Toad Sr. and the advertisers. " Hedgehog decided to continue to withhold the fact that Toad Sr. had threatened to shut them down.

Rabbit let out an audible harrumph.

"It sounds as though you have something to say, Rabbit," Hedgehog said. Rabbit was the newspaper's editor in chief. Hedgehog had worked with Rabbit for years at *The Meadowvale Tribune* and had brought her over when *The Gazette*'s long time editor retired. He deeply respected her opinion, and if she had something to say, he wanted to hear it.

"We've already cut costs to the bone," Rabbit said. "If we want to grow, we need to invest money, not make cuts. I have a chance to hire Suzy Sparrow as a finance writer. Our readers have been asking for more articles on money management, and she would be perfect. We need to expand the paper, not shrink it. If we have to shrink editorial, we might as well shut down the paper."

Rabbit and Toad Sr. had very different perspectives and yet they were both entertaining the idea of closing the paper. For the first time in his career, Hedgehog wondered if all of the hype about the death of the newspaper might have some validity. He regretted buying such a large house. It was expensive to finance and would take a long time to sell if things did not work out at *The Gazette*.

"Well, I certainly can't cut costs," Badger, the production director, said in a gruff tone. "Newsprint costs what it costs. Ink costs what it costs. And we need the guys we have to run the presses. The only thing we can do is get rid of the TV schedule. That thing is a nightmare to print."

"No!" said Squirrel and Deer simultaneously.

"Every time we change anything in the TV schedule, the switchboard lights up with calls from subscribers wanting to yell at me and cancel their subscriptions," said Deer, who managed circulation. "You'd be amazed at how important the TV schedule is to some animals. Some animals plan their whole week around the television schedule."

"Old animals," Toad Jr. said. The 25-year-old head of promotions, and son of Toad Sr., was leaning back in his chair with neon-green designer sneakers propped up on the boardroom table. "Who watches TV anymore? All my friends are streaming things on the Web or using MooTube."

"I watch TV," Deer snapped. "And based on the number of subscriber complaints I get when there is a misprint in the television guide, I'd venture to say that almost everyone reading our paper watches TV, too."

"Exactly my point," Toad Jr. said. "The newspaper business is dying. No offense, but our audience seems to consist of a bunch of senior citizens who are not embracing technology. Who wants to reach them? Not the makers of smart phones or running shoes or other forward-looking advertisers. We would be so much better off if we just had an online version of the paper. We'd be more relevant and could break stories instead of printing day-old information. We'd attract younger readers. We'd have lower overall costs. *The Left Fauna Post* does not even pay its writers."

"And it shows!" Rabbit protested. "They don't even fact-check. They are constantly running obituaries for famous creatures who are still alive!"

"They have over a million daily readers and were just acquired for $250 million," said Toad Jr.

"That doesn't make what they do okay," said Rabbit. "We have certain journalistic principles to uphold!"

"Who says?" asked Owl. Everyone turned to face her. Owl rarely participated in meetings unless she was asked a direct question about the numbers.

Owl's feathers fluffed up, revealing her embarrassment at being the center of attention. "Look, I'm all in favor of principles, and I don't know the answer to our problems, but I know that every month our numbers stay flat—or get worse. We are all working hard and yet it's not enough. It's time to do something different. Maybe we should think about what Toad Jr. is proposing. It makes a lot of sense to me."

Hedgehog looked at the group. "Squirrel, do you have anything to add? You've been uncharacteristically quiet," he said.

"I wanted to gather more information before I said anything. I want to research the market a bit more. Anecdotally, advertising customers are pushing for lower pricing. One of my clients, Turtle, from

Turtle Travel, said that he can run an online advertising campaign for 5 percent of what he spends with us. I have no idea how to compete with that," Squirrel said.

"But are the animals reading his ads good prospects?" Rabbit asked. "We have highly educated readers with a bit of disposable income. That's worth more than a bunch of random creatures surfing around the web."

Squirrel shrugged. "Turtle says he's moved a lot of cheap trips to Sunny Island over the Internet. Maybe he's selling to less sophisticated buyers, but I'm not sure he cares. And he can expand his reach beyond Toad Hollow and connect with communities that weren't hit as hard by the recession."

"So are you saying that perhaps we don't want to be a newspaper anymore?" Hedgehog asked, remembering his conversation with Fox.

"Newspapers are dying," declared Toad Jr.

Rabbit shook her head angrily.

Hedgehog's natural inclination was to side with Rabbit. He believed that newspapers were not a dying medium. There would always be creatures who wanted to flip through a physical paper at the breakfast table or read one on the train. Creatures would always want to cut out an article and send it to a friend. Without paid investigative reporters, who would keep animals honest, or blow the whistle on corporate and political corruption? Hedgehog could not imagine a world without traditional media, but perhaps Toad Jr. was right. Maybe he was a dinosaur too. Maybe young creatures no longer cared.

"Dog?" Hedgehog asked. Dog ran Animal Resources and Hedgehog wanted to understand the AR implications. Dog was also very good at seeing things from a number of points of view.

"Staff cuts would be terrible for morale, plus there would be upfront costs associated with severance packages," Dog said. "And any change in our business would require training for our employees.

It all costs money that is not in my current budget. I think that we need to involve a lot more creatures in the discussion. What does Toad Sr. want us to do? What does the board want? What do readers want to read?"

Hedgehog had no idea. He felt stuck. There were no good options to present to the board before Friday.

"What if we shrunk the paper by 15 percent?" Hedgehog asked Owl and Badger.

"That would result in some cost savings in terms of paper and ink," Badger said. "I could probably get rid of two workers. A couple of the chickens are nearing retirement."

Owl and Dog nodded in agreement

"Exactly what content would we cut?" Rabbit asked.

"I'd leave that up to you," Hedgehog said.

"Readership surveys indicate that the creatures of Toad Hollow most want to read articles on how to navigate this post-recessionary world. They want more information about how to budget, how to pay down their debts, and how to earn more money. Hiring Suzy Sparrow would help us give our readers what we need, but I take it you don't want to entertain any ideas that increase content," Rabbit said sourly.

"I'd hold off on hiring anyone until we figure this out," Hedgehog said.

Rabbit folded her front paws in front of her and leaned back in her chair a little, indicating that as far as she was concerned, this meeting was over.

Hedgehog hated the tension in the room, but it was clear that there were not going to be any solutions that would please everyone. Meetings only ever caused a lot of trouble. Fox was wrong: Involving the pack was a bad idea.

"Toad Jr., what is the one thing we could do right now that would increase our digital presence?" Hedgehog asked, trying to get things back on track.

"All the columnists need to be online and posting stuff daily," Toad Jr. said.

"They are busy chasing down stories!" Rabbit protested. "They don't have time to be Tweeting."

"It would be good for their brand." Toad Jr. said. "Those working on books could promote them. We can monitor who is reading their columns and know who is being read. We could pay the popular columnists more and get rid of the unpopular ones. Right now we have no way of knowing who the popular columnists even are!"

"That's not true," Rabbit said. "We have letters to the editor and reader surveys."

"Which tell us nothing," Toad Jr. said.

"Are you going to let the promotions guy dictate editorial policy?" Rabbit asked Hedgehog.

Toad Jr. jumped in before Hedgehog could respond: "Look, I know that my reputation here is that I'm the oddball son of the founder. But I have a business degree from Vale University and among the many jobs I've held—and yes, I've held far too many—I've worked on two digital startups that were sold for a lot of money. Plus, I sold that energy drink company I founded to a national label. I'm here because I think I can help you and I'd like to see the business my family built survive."

Hedgehog had never heard Toad Jr. speak this way. He thought he was a spoiled brat but perhaps their interests were more aligned than he had thought.

"What are we going to do about the discounts?" Squirrel asked, changing the topic. "Raccoon Auto Mart, Big Bear Real Estate, Turtle Travel and Magpie Jewelers want an answer by Friday . . ."

"Magpie has a big mouth. If you give him a discount, you'll have to give it to everyone," Badger said bitterly. When Badger had gone into Magpie's jewelry store to look—just look—at engagement rings for his then girlfriend, Magpie had told a couple of creatures about it over drinks. Word got around to his girlfriend, and when he did not propose to her on her birthday, as she had expected, she broke up with him.

Hedgehog's head was spinning. He wished that he could talk to Cindy, his wife.

"Let's try to keep everyone on hold. I don't want to decide anything today," Hedgehog said. "I think that we need some time to think about what we discussed."

"I can't keep them on hold forever. I'll need to get back to the advertisers tomorrow," said Squirrel.

"And Suzy Sparrow. Should I tell her that we are no longer interested?" Rabbit asked pointedly. "Should I get the columnists to contact Toad Jr. about setting up blogs? And when do you need to know what content I'm cutting?"

"I'll need a budget if I'm taking the paper online," Toad Jr. said. "It's cheaper than print but it's not free."

"So will I," said Coyote, the information systems director who'd been observing the conversation. "Every time Toad Jr. uploads a new video about that starlet Maggie Muskrat, our servers crash. We will need a systems overhaul if we are moving more content online. We need to put things up in the cloud."

"And if I need to be telling two of the chickens they are retiring early because we don't need so many guys on the presses, I should do that sooner rather than later," said Badger. "They have always wanted to go south over the winter and would appreciate the opportunity to stay longer."

"I'll need to start preparing a retirement package if that's the case," said Dog.

"And I need to give Rat at the bank a status update if we are incurring one-time costs like severance payments and a systems upgrade. They might impact our loan agreement," said Owl. "I'll need to get numbers from Squirrel, Rabbit, Dog, and Badger to revise my projections for the year."

Hedgehog wished he were the one retiring. There were a lot of issues that needed to be resolved. And it was clear, from the tone of the meeting, that no one decision would please everyone. Anything that made Toad Jr. happy would anger Rabbit. And while he had a huge loyalty to Rabbit for following him to *The Gazette* from *The Meadowvale Tribune*, he knew that angering Toad Jr.—and thereby angering Toad Sr.—could end his career.

Hedgehog adjourned the meeting and promised everyone that he'd follow up with them tomorrow. He asked everyone to be ready for a management meeting the next day at two o'clock. He then went back to his office and asked Fieldmouse to edit and print off the minutes as soon as possible. He wanted to make sure he was on top of everything they'd discussed.

Hedgehog ate lunch at his desk. He wanted to read over all of the information and did not feel like talking to anyone in the cafeteria. His management team seemed content to avoid him as well. The impending cuts were breeding a sense of fear. Everyone was busy in their offices going through their own numbers and getting their proverbial ducks in a row.

Toward the end of the day, Hedgehog heard a soft knock on his door. It was Rabbit.

Hedgehog motioned for her to come in.

"Hey, what's up?" he asked.

Rabbit closed the door behind her and took a seat.

"Hedgehog, I just wanted to let you know that I've been offered a job with *The Bramblethorn Banner* and I think I'm going to take it," she said.

Hedgehog was stunned. "I, um, I did not know that you were looking for another job, Rabbit," he said.

"I wasn't," Rabbit said. "They've been asking me to join them for years. I would have taken their offer had you not asked me to join you here at *The Gazette*. But Hedgehog, you know that the job has not exactly turned out the way I thought it would. Toad Sr. is still too involved. He won't let me do any investigative stuff that might embarrass his friends. When Weasel sold off that big piece of the forest to those developers it was an important story. But we had to kill it because Toad Sr. and Weasel are friends. *The Bramblethorn Banner* has promised to give me a lot more freedom. I'd have a big budget and could hire Suzy Sparrow and other writers I want. Plus they flew me and my husband and all of our bunnies down there one weekend to check things out. They gave us floor seats at the basketball game, which impressed my husband and the bunnies. And one of my favorite cousins lives there with her family. But even with all that, I'd never really considered the offer until today. I believe in newspapers, Hedgehog. I believe that the creatures of Toad Hollow deserve better than reading something off the newswire or the rant of some uninformed amateur. I believe in education and I think that newspapers can educate creatures to be better versions of themselves. But I just don't think that *The Gazette* is headed in a direction I like."

"But *The Bramblethorn Banner* is another newspaper, Rabbit," Hedgehog said. "I know that, as a community, Bramblethorn is not facing the same dire economic conditions as Toad Hollow but the *Banner* is still a newspaper and soon will be facing the same pressures that the entire industry is facing."

"I talked at length with their publisher about that very thing," Rabbit said. "The last thing I want to do is to go from the frying pan into the fire. They have expanded their editorial department to reach international readers. They have established a paywall so the print content can be read online for a fee. They have made a firm commitment to remain a newspaper. I think I'd fit in better there."

"Rabbit. I don't know what to say," Hedgehog said. "Is your decision final?"

"I just got off the phone with the publisher and he wants to know by Monday," Rabbit said. "Look, I don't want there to be any hard feelings and I want you to make the decisions you need to make. Maybe Toad Jr. is right. It's hard to argue with online news sites getting $250-million-dollar buyouts. But that business is not for me."

"Can you give me a couple of weeks to get things figured out?" Hedgehog asked.

"Only until Monday," Rabbit said. "I made a promise to the Bramblethorn guys. But I won't make my final decision until then."

"Thank you," Hedgehog said sincerely.

In a way, Rabbit had just given him a big gift. She had removed the conflict from the decision and had indirectly given him her blessing to move the business online using a lower-cost production model. But was this the right decision to make?

Fieldmouse poked his head in Hedgehog's office.

"It's Toad Sr.," he said.

"Put him through," Hedgehog sighed.

"What's going on?" Toad Sr. demanded.

"We just had a management meeting to talk about some options," Hedgehog said.

"Toad Jr. said it was more like a bun fight," said Toad Sr. "It doesn't sound like you resolved anything. Did you tell these people that their jobs are on the line?"

"Are they?" Hedgehog asked bluntly.

Toad Sr. let out a deep sigh. "Look, Hedgehog. I like you. I know you don't think I do, but I do. I know that most of the things that have happened to this paper are not your fault. I'm not stupid. I know the industry is in decline and I know Toad Hollow has been hit harder than most other towns. But that's the point. I need to put my money into something that is going to succeed. If newspapers have run their course, then I need to pull out now. It worries me when I hear reports that the most creative idea you have is to cut costs. So yes, if we lose these four advertisers, I will shut down the paper. And if the only way we can keep these four advertisers is to give them deep discounts and then cut costs to the bone, I will also shut things down. I thought that if I was gruff, I could shock you into action, but perhaps you are just not the right guy for the job."

"Will you give me time to fix this?" Hedgehog asked.

"You have until the end of business tomorrow to come up with a solution for our advertisers. Let's talk then and see where things stand," Toad Sr. said. His tone had softened considerably. Strangely, Hedgehog preferred it when he was yelling.

"Okay," Hedgehog said.

"Do you know why I hired you?" Toad Sr. asked.

"Because I saved so much money when I ran operations at *The Meadowvale Tribune*?" Hedgehog asked.

"Nope," Toad Sr. stated. "It's because I read your coverage of the Elephant/Tiger War." Early in his career, Hedgehog had been stationed overseas, writing mining reports for a business journal when a war had broken out between the Elephants and the Tigers, who had only a tenuous peace treaty. Since he was one of the few journalists in the area, his coverage of the war got picked up by all of the international papers. It made his career.

"Oh," said Hedgehog. "I wrote that series so long ago. I thought you liked my administrative capabilities."

"I did," said Toad Sr., "but there are lots of capable administrators out there. I wanted to hire the guy who was hired to write some boring mining reports but who, when faced with a war, got into the heart of the action and found a way to get the story heard. You interviewed Desert Fox, one of the greatest military leaders of our time."

Desert Fox was a famous military leader whose creative approach to battle de-escalated a number of potentially violent situations when the interspecies peace treaties were first signed.

"You hired me because I met Desert Fox?" Hedgehog asked.

"I hired you because you clearly learned from Desert Fox. You went from being a desk clerk to being so committed to getting your story that you got wounded in battle."

Hedgehog had been shot in the leg during a battle. He was sent home to Meadowvale where he met Cindy, who was working in the hospital as a physiotherapist.

"I knew that if anyone could turn this mess of a paper around, it would be you. That's why I've been trying to shout at you like a drill sergeant," said Toad Sr. "I don't have much time, but I'm giving you carte blanche. Tell me what we can do to turn this thing around. You didn't let the fact that you were a mining reporter keep you out of the action overseas. Don't be held back by the limitations of the newspaper business. We don't have to play by those rules." Toad hung up the phone, gently this time.

Hedgehog thought about his recent encounter with a different kind of fox. Perhaps this is what Fox had been trying to tell him when he asked him if the newspaper needed to be a newspaper. Yesterday, Hedgehog thought he was crazy but perhaps it made sense.

Hedgehog walked over to the hook on the back of his door where he had hung his jacket and pulled Fox's business card out of the pocket.

He dialed the number.

"Fox speaking," said the voice from the bar.

"Hey, Fox, it's Hedgehog. You know, from the Tipsy Marmot Tavern in Toad Hollow," Hedgehog said.

"Oh, yes. Hello, Hedgehog. Of course I remember you," said Fox. "Glad you called."

"Say, you don't happen to have dinner plans tonight, do you?" Hedgehog asked. "I want to find out more about your consulting services."

# CHAPTER THREE

# FOX'S THINKING PROCESS

"What do you mean, you've engaged a fox?" asked Fieldmouse, looking up from his computer.

After last evening's dinner, Hedgehog had been so impressed with Fox that he'd hired him on the spot to do some consulting. Fox's work with his other client had gone better than expected and they had wrapped up a day early. He did not have to be at the airport until Friday evening and had agreed to spend the day with Hedgehog. Hedgehog had asked Fieldmouse to clear his schedule until the management meeting at two o'clock.

"I've engaged a consultant to help me take a look at all of the issues we have," Hedgehog said.

"You need to give Toad and the advertisers an answer by the end of the day," Fieldmouse reminded him.

"That's still the plan," Hedgehog said. "And I think this guy can help us. I'll need you to hold all my calls this morning. I can talk to Rabbit or Toad Sr. if it's urgent, but everyone else will have to wait."

"Is that a good idea?" Fieldmouse asked. "I have heard rumors that there might be layoffs. The staff is worried. If they see you disappearing into a boardroom with some strange fox, they might panic."

"If I don't get some time this morning to go over the issues, then there will be a reason to panic. I'm trying to avoid that," Hedgehog said.

"Fine, I'll hold your calls," sighed Fieldmouse.

Hedgehog was about to leave when he noticed something on Fieldmouse's desk. He pointed to the book titled *Supersymmetry and String Theory: Beyond the Standard Model.*

"String theory. Isn't that advanced physics?" Hedgehog asked.

"It is!" said Fieldmouse. "It's a theoretical framework to understand particle physics better. Are you a science buff? "

"Not particularly," Hedgehog said, making a mental note to research the subject when he had time. Fieldmouse seemed like such a quiet fellow, yet he'd been holding court at the Poetry Slam at the Smiling Moose Café the other evening. Clearly there were sides to him that Hedgehog did not see at work.

A few minutes after Hedgehog returned to his desk there was a knock on his door. It was Fox. Once again, he looked as though he'd just stepped out of the pages of a catalog.

"Good morning!" he said cheerfully.

"Um, good morning," said Hedgehog, somewhat surprised that the receptionist—a rather surly woodchuck—had let Fox in without calling him to confirm the appointment.

"Your charming receptionist told me I'd find you here," he said. "Is now a good time for you?"

Hedgehog, stunned at the notion that anyone might find Woodchuck charming, nodded and invited him to take a seat in one of the velvet club chairs.

Fox let out a long whistle. "Cozy chairs," he commented. "You could spend all day in here."

"And sometimes all night, too." Hedgehog said.

"No rest for the wicked," Fox laughed. He pulled a laptop out of his bag and switched it on. "I'll be taking a few notes," he said.

"So you can come up with the answers I need, I hope," Hedgehog said.

Fox shook his head. "Remember, you don't need me to come up with answers. You need me to come up with questions."

Hedgehog laughed nervously. "I hope I'm not paying you for questions. As I mentioned last night over dinner, questions I've got. Should we discount advertising for everyone? Should we have a bigger online presence? Should we trim the number of pages to cut costs? Should I make Rabbit a better offer to keep her as our editor?"

Fox smiled. "Let me rephrase that. You need me to come up with the *right* questions."

"Nope, I need you to come up with the right *answers*," Hedgehog said firmly. Maybe this had been a bad idea.

There was a knock on the door. It was Squirrel. "Just a minute," Hedgehog said, "It's my advertising director. I'm going to tell him to come back later. Fieldmouse was supposed to keep everyone away."

"No, please have him come in. I insist," Fox said.

Hedgehog shook his head.

"It's part of the consulting process," Fox said. "Please, have him come in."

Hedgehog hesitantly waved Squirrel into the office.

"Hello," said Squirrel, breathlessly.

Fox shook Squirrel's paw.

"Squirrel, this is Fox, a consultant I've hired to help us. Fox, this is Squirrel, our director of advertising."

"Hello, Fox." Squirrel said. "Sorry to bother you, Hedgehog, but I just wanted to let you know that I've heard from Turtle, Bear, and Magpie this morning. They are all demanding the same discount that Raccoon is. I know this is not new information, but I wanted to let you know that they told me what they told Toad Sr. yesterday."

"Did they call as a group?" asked Fox.

Squirrel looked at Hedgehog, who nodded. "It's okay. I've briefed him on what's going on."

"They called individually. But their requests were pretty similar," Squirrel said.

"Did you tell them that they are locked into a contract for another year?" Hedgehog asked.

"I did," said Squirrel. "And they all talked about how we have not upheld our end of the deal. Clearly, they've been talking to their lawyers. I'm going back to crunch those numbers you need for our meeting this afternoon but I wanted to let you know." Squirrel left Hedgehog's office.

Hedgehog sighed. "I don't think we have any alternative to giving them a discount. The Internet is forcing our prices down," Hedgehog said.

"So why don't you simply extend the discount right away? If you have to do it, then why is there any doubt? Why am I here?" Fox asked.

"Well, I don't want to do it. It will destroy our financial results. But I can't risk losing our top four advertisers. Toad Sr. will shut us down." Hedgehog said.

"From what you said at dinner, Toad Sr. is going to shut you down no matter what you do. So again, why hire me?" Fox asked.

"I can only see a rock and a hard place," said Hedgehog. "I guess I'm hoping that you see something I don't."

"Why is Squirrel not responsible for making this decision?" Fox asked. "Doesn't he manage the relationship with the advertisers?"

"I like to be the final authority on big decisions," Hedgehog said. "I'm the one with the big performance clause in my contract. If Squirrel screws up, I get fired."

"That's a lot of pressure on you and on Squirrel," Fox said.

"Well, that's why I get so involved," said Hedgehog.

"So what's your relationship with, say, Turtle?" Fox asked. "How long has he been a client? What is his annual advertising spend? How much other business do you attract because he advertises with you? How soon after receiving an invoice does he pay? Has he ever asked for a discount before? Has he ever threatened to pull his business? How trustworthy is he?"

"I don't know," Hedgehog said. "I'd have to ask Squirrel."

"I see," said Fox.

"I guess that sounds stupid, right? He has all the information and I'm making the decisions."

"Why do you think you have to offer the discount?" Fox asked.

"Our advertisers think our industry is dying and know we are at their mercy. They can get ads much cheaper online," Hedgehog explained.

"So, is this the most important decision facing you right now?" Fox asked.

Hedgehog nodded.

"May I use your white board?" Fox asked.

Hedgehog nodded again.

Fox went over to the white board and uncapped the marker. He wrote: *Decide on Ad Discount.*

"What else?" he asked.

"Well, if I give the ad discount to those four advertisers then I may have to pass on the discount to others. There are no secrets in a town like Toad Hollow. So, basically I have to decide on an ad price strategy for the future," Hedgehog said.

Fox wrote: *Decide Ad Price Strategy.*

"Anything else?" Fox asked.

"Well," Hedgehog continued, "I don't see ad prices going up, so we need to look at where we can trim costs. Toad Sr. has made it clear that he'll shut us down if profits dip any further."

Fox wrote: *Reduce Costs.*

"The price of newsprint and ink are what they are," continued

Hedgehog, "so we can either look at decreasing the size of the paper or having fewer employees produce the paper. Either way trims labor costs, which is what we have to do."

Fox amended *Reduce Costs* to read: *Reduce Labor Costs and/or Shrink Paper.*

"Rabbit has told me she will be taking another job on Monday unless I can promise her that she won't be affected by any changes we may decide to make, so I guess I'll have to find a new editor," Hedgehog said.

Fox wrote: *Find New Editor.*

"Is that everything?" Fox asked.

Hedgehog nodded.

Fox stepped back to look at the whiteboard.

---

*Decide on Ad Discount*
*Decide Ad Price Strategy*
*Reduce Labor Costs and/or Shrink Paper*
*Find New Editor*

---

Fox pointed at the whiteboard. "Do you see what's wrong with this picture?" he asked.

Hedgehog nodded. "I know. It's impossible," he moaned.

"Who runs this newspaper?" Fox asked.

"Well, I guess I do," Hedgehog said. "Toad Sr. and the Board do as well, but I'm responsible for most of it."

"So then why are you letting Raccoon do your work?" asked Fox.

"What do you mean?" asked Hedgehog.

"Was it not Raccoon asking for a discounted ad rate that set this whole thing in motion?" Fox clarified.

"It was," said Hedgehog.

"So Raccoon asks for a discount and within two days you have decided to discount all ads, reduce labor costs, and allow Rabbit—one of the best editors in the business—to go work for the competition.

You've decided to concede your business and jump on board the Internet train, without looking at any other alternatives. Sounds to me like Raccoon is running your business," Fox said.

Hedgehog paused. "Raccoon is representative of what all our customers are going to be doing eventually. We are being made obsolete. I'd be silly not to make these changes. As a consultant, I thought you'd embrace change. I thought you'd understand."

"What does your sales guy have to say about this? Or production director? What about AR? What about the board of directors?" Fox asked.

"Well, of course I'm going to get their opinions before I act on this," Hedgehog protested.

"But you're already acting on this," Fox said. "You have jumped to a conclusion that the ad discount is necessary, and now are going about gathering evidence that supports the thesis that your industry is in a decline."

"But everybody knows that the newspaper is a dying medium," said Hedgehog. "It's not like I'm making this stuff up! Haven't you read *Hogsford Business Review*? We are all facing a decline."

"I know that you know your business, but that can work against you," Fox said. "The brain is an amazing thing. It's capable of holding a lot of information but it has some basic pitfalls. For example, generally, we hate to lose. In fact, we would rather forfeit a potential gain if it meant risking a loss. This is why so many creatures make mistakes with their money. It can also lead to bad decisions in business. You'd rather give away 15 percent of your margin than risk losing a client that you might lose at some future date anyway."

"Is that the only trap?" Hedgehog asked.

"Nope, there are lots. Another key trap is that our brains like to look for patterns, and sometimes we confuse correlation—two things happening at the same time—with cause—one thing happening because of another. We often make assumptions about what is happening and we jump to conclusions about how to resolve issues.

The Internet is gaining in popularity and your numbers are down. Do you know with certainty that the Internet caused the decline?"

"So you don't think we need to move to an Internet-based model?" Hedgehog asked.

"I don't know. The question I'd ask you is why adopt an Internet model? Why not change your business entirely and become a pickle factory?" Fox asked.

"Because we are a newspaper, not a pickle factory. We don't know the first thing about pickles. Lots of newspapers have gone online. None have become pickle factories," Hedgehog snapped. He had to come up with a solution to appease the advertisers and get Toad Sr. to reconsider closing the paper and this guy was talking to him about pickle factories!

"I'm not saying that you should be a pickle factory. I'm just saying that you need to think critically about your direction rather than react to outward circumstances. You need to gather some more information, generate some other alternatives, and evaluate those alternatives. You also need to get employees on board with whatever decision you make."

"You can help me do that in the next four hours?" Hedgehog asked.

"I can," Fox said. "And then once I've shown you what to do, you can do it on your own for other decisions."

"What's the first step?" Hedgehog asked, mindful of the time. He had a lot of decisions to make in the next few days.

"Well," Fox continued, "it can be very helpful to have a basic thinking process in place to help you avoid some of these pitfalls and make better decisions. This is mine."

He reached into his messenger bag and pulled out a laminated card.

"Here is a quick summary card of the process. But don't worry about understanding it yet," Fox said, handing the card to Hedgehog:

## Critical Thinking Process

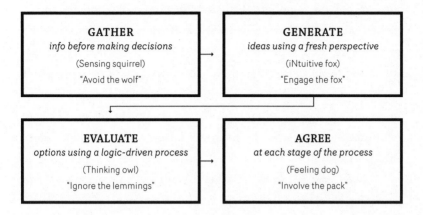

Hedgehog turned the card over to reveal the back:

## Critical Thinking Skills for Issues Management

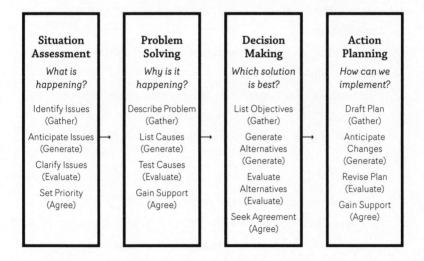

Hedgehog smiled. "Ah, the two-by-two matrix," he said.

"You hire a consultant, you get a two-by-two matrix. Union rules," Fox laughed. "The critical thinking process boils down to four simple steps: gather, generate, evaluate, agree. If you do these four things, you can think through any issue you face. To make sure I don't leave out a step, I put together a little memory trick. Back when animals used to eat one another, geese ate fish and insects. I remember seeing an old photo of a protest march and a cricket was holding a placard saying Good Geese Eat Apples. The saying stuck in my brain. It can help you remember that when we are thinking critically about an issue, we must Gather information, Generate ideas, Evaluate solutions, and Agree on the best way forward. GGEA. Good Geese Eat Apples."

"Good Geese Eat Apples. Gather, Generate, Evaluate, Agree. I can remember that!" said Hedgehog.

"Great!" Fox continued, "First, we *gather* the facts to ensure that we have all of the necessary information. Next, we *generate* possible solutions and alternatives. Third, we *evaluate* the information to figure out what action we wish to take. Finally, we seek *agreement* within the organization to build commitment and support for implementation."

"So for every decision, I have to do this?" Hedgehog asked. "That sounds impossible!"

Fox laughed. "Believe me, this will become second nature."

"I suppose," Hedgehog said skeptically.

Fox looked at his watch. "Do you want to grab a coffee before we continue?"

"Sure," Hedgehog said.

"Okay, now what thoughts went into that decision?" Fox asked.

"Decision?" Hedgehog asked.

"The decision that you want to get a coffee," Fox said.

"None," Hedgehog said. "I just really like coffee."

"Are you sure that's all?" Fox pressed. "What if I asked you if you wanted a coffee while you were holding a fresh cup of coffee in your hand?"

"I'd think you were nuts. Why would I want a coffee if I had a coffee?" Hedgehog said.

"So in other words, how much coffee you've had and how recently you've had it informs your decision somehow," Fox confirmed.

"I guess," Hedgehog said, wondering where this was leading.

"So, what other things might your brain have considered to arrive at your very fast yes to that cup of coffee?" Fox asked.

"Okay," Hedgehog said, trying to play along. "I have not had any coffee since 7:00 a.m., and I suspect it will be a long day and night so I need to be caffeinated. Plus, my stomach is rumbling and I'd like a muffin. Given how complicated this all seems, it may be a while before we get lunch. All that led to yes."

"So, in other words, you gathered the facts: you have not had coffee since 7:00 a.m. and you are hungry. You generated some ideas: You could get a muffin along with your coffee. You evaluated the idea: You have not had too much caffeine or too many calories today. And you already knew I'd likely agree since I made the suggestion. Do you see? Gather, Generate, Evaluate, Agree. Good Geese Eat Apples. You did it in under five seconds."

## Critical Thinking Process

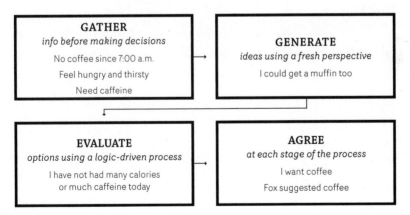

| GATHER | GENERATE |
|---|---|
| *info before making decisions* | *ideas using a fresh perspective* |
| No coffee since 7:00 a.m. | I could get a muffin too |
| Feel hungry and thirsty | |
| Need caffeine | |

| EVALUATE | AGREE |
|---|---|
| *options using a logic-driven process* | *at each stage of the process* |
| I have not had many calories or much caffeine today | I want coffee |
| | Fox suggested coffee |

"And how do you know that I didn't do that with the ad decision?" Hedgehog asked.

"Well, because you seem a lot more miserable about the ad

decision than about the coffee. When you run through a decision process properly, you tend to be confident about moving forward. Plus, given how important the ad decision is, and all the things that may flow from it, the decision ought to take longer than deciding on a cup of coffee. Right?" Fox asked.

Hedgehog nodded.

Fox continued. "The nice thing about using a simple thinking process is that you can quickly determine if you have enough information to comfortably proceed with your decision. If not, you feel more comfortable asking for more time to run through the process. That's when having well-developed critical thinking skills such as situation assessment, problem solving, decision making, and action planning can be very useful."

"But I have to make a decision now!" Hedgehog said. "My advertisers and Toad Sr. want to hear back from me by the end of the day."

"Don't worry, they will," Fox said. "Now let's get that coffee."

"That wasn't just a technique?" asked Hedgehog.

"Coffee is never just a technique!" Fox said.

"I'll get Fieldmouse to bring us some—and two muffins" said Hedgehog.

"Great," said Fox. "While we are waiting, we can go over the critical thinking process in more detail."

# CHAPTER FOUR

# REMEMBER THE SQUIRREL: GATHERING INFORMATION

Hedgehog looked at the card Fox had given him.

### Critical Thinking Process

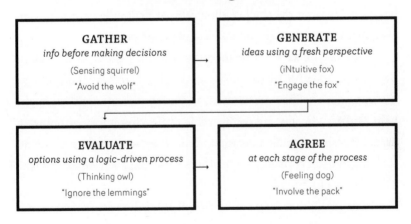

| GATHER | GENERATE |
|---|---|
| *info before making decisions* | *ideas using a fresh perspective* |
| (Sensing squirrel) | (iNtuitive fox) |
| "Avoid the wolf" | "Engage the fox" |

| EVALUATE | AGREE |
|---|---|
| *options using a logic-driven process* | *at each stage of the process* |
| (Thinking owl) | (Feeling dog) |
| "Ignore the lemmings" | "Involve the pack" |

"Let's focus on the first step in the process," Fox said

| GATHER |
|---|
| *info before making decisions* |
| (Sensing squirrel) |
| "Avoid the wolf" |

"Did you customize this chart for us?" Hedgehog asked. "You have Squirrel's name there."

"Let me explain," said Fox. "Have you ever had a Myers-Briggs Type Indicator® profile done?"

"Is that like being a Pisces or having your colors done?" Hedgehog asked. "I think I'm a Spring."

Fox chuckled. "Not exactly," he said. "The Myers-Briggs Type Indicator®, or MBTI®, is a tool that helps you understand your inborn preferences. You are asked a series of questions that help reveal what energizes you, how you prefer to acquire information, how you process that information, and whether you like to evaluate that information to reach a decision quickly or remain open to possibilities. The assessment will give you a four letter description like ISTJ or ENFP."

"Oh, yes," Hedgehog said. "The AR guys at *The Meadowvale Tribune* got us all to do that as part of a team-building exercise," Hedgehog said. He went over to his filing cabinet and pulled out a drawer. He quickly rifled though some files and pulled one out.

"Eureka!" he said. He opened the file and pulled out a piece of paper. "I'm an ISTJ," he said.

Fox nodded. "That description, assuming you agree with it, might help explain why you are comfortable evaluating information; were uncomfortable making a decision about Raccoon before you had all the data; did not consult your business partners; and wanted to make a decision right away."

"You got all that from four letters?" Hedgehog asked.

Fox nodded. "The letters denote your preferred style of collecting and analyzing information, making decisions and relating to the world at large."

"What do you mean by preferred style?" asked Hedgehog.

"Are you right- or left-pawed?" Fox asked.

"Right," Hedgehog answered.

"If I asked you to sign a check using your left paw, could you do it?" Fox asked.

"I could, but it would feel awkward and it might be illegible," Hedgehog said.

"That's sort of how our preferences work. We are naturally more comfortable in some areas," Fox said.

"I'm rarely comfortable when signing a check," Hedgehog said dryly.

"For the purpose of our critical thinking matrix, I want to focus on the middle two letters of the Myers-Briggs profile," Fox said.

"The S and the T?" Hedgehog asked.

"In your case, yes," Fox confirmed. "MBTI looks at the two ways most creatures like to collect information: through sensing or through intuition. The S from your Myers-Briggs profile indicates that you have a preference for sensing. When it comes to sourcing information, animals with a preference for sensing tend to gather data and facts. They lean on their senses and prefer information that can be verified by sight, smell, touch, taste, or sound. They like clear evidence, experience-based information, and details. This is exactly what is required for the first step of the thinking process. Since I'm a big fan of memory tricks, I like to think of a squirrel gathering up nuts for the winter when I think of this step."

"Sounds like Squirrel, our head of advertising sales," Hedgehog said. "I got mad at him because he did not come to me as soon as he heard that Raccoon wanted a discount, but he did not feel comfortable approaching me until he had gathered more information."

"Sounds like he might be a senser. What makes him a good sales guy?" Fox asked.

"Hmm," said Hedgehog, thinking. "Squirrel understands his ad customers in detail. He will ask me what features we are working on and then sell ads that work well with our content. He always knows what his expenses and revenues are. Owl, our finance director, has told me that whenever she asks Squirrel for financial projections, he peppers her with a million questions until he understands exactly what data she is looking for. "

"Sensers, like you and Squirrel, are great animals to have at the beginning of the thinking process as you gather information," Fox observed. "Sensers tend to love facts and data. They want to be able to prove everything by questioning assumptions and grounding any assertions with research. It's what they do best. That's why you were not comfortable making a snap decision. You had not done your homework yet."

"So are you saying that in order to make decisions, I have to do a Myers-Briggs profile on everyone?" Hedgehog asked.

"Great question," Fox said, "and the answer is no. Knowing someone's natural tendencies can be useful in any endeavor requiring teamwork, but it is not necessary. I'm not saying that you need to know that you have a senser on your team to gather information. What I am saying is that when you are faced with a decision, you need to have the animals involved tap into their inner squirrel. This will be more comfortable for some animals than for others."

Hedgehog pointed at the card. "Avoid the wolf?" he asked.

"With each of the steps in the thinking process, there are potential pitfalls. These are errors a lot of creatures make at this step. Knowing what might trip you up at each stage of the process can help you stay out of trouble."

"So we are to avoid wolves?" Hedgehog asked.

"Metaphorically, yes," Fox said. "Did your mother ever read you Aesop's fables when you were a hoglet?"

Hedgehog nodded, "Like 'The Fox and the Grapes' and 'The Tortoise and the Hare'?"

"Exactly. Ever hear the one about 'The Wolf and the Lamb'?" Fox asked.

Hedgehog shook his head.

"Well, let me tell it to you," Fox said. "It illustrates one of the traps we often fall into when gathering information:

*A long time ago, before the peace treaty, a wolf was drinking out of a stream on a hillside. He saw a tasty-looking little lamb having a drink farther downstream. The wolf knew that eating other animals was falling out of favor, but he was hungry and was hoping that he could find a reason to justify eating the lamb.*

*He called out to the lamb, "Lamb, you got mud in my drinking water! You need to be punished."*

*The lamb, who was downstream, said, "You're mistaken. The water runs downstream from you to me so there is no way that I could have muddied it."*

*The wolf, still hungry, said, "You look a lot like the lamb who was telling lies about me last summer. I have a right to defend my reputation."*

*The lamb responded. "I have not told any lies about you. Besides, I am only six months old. Last summer, I'd not been born."*

*"Well," said the wolf, "If it was not you, it was your father who was spreading lies. And I must take my revenge."*

*With that, the wolf came and gobbled up the lamb for his dinner.*

Hedgehog was horrified, "My mother never told me that story. So am I supposed to be the wolf or the lamb?" he asked.

Fox laughed. "When it comes to critical thinking, we all tend to be the wolf," he said. "Most of us fail to gather the information we need to make a good decision. Like the wolf, we jump to a conclusion, usually based on desire and emotion. In the wolf's case, he was hungry and figured that the only solution was to eat the lamb. He needed to justify his actions and tried to gather the evidence to prove that the lamb deserved to be eaten," Fox said.

"So in this case, are you saying that I want to give a discount to our advertisers and am trying to justify it? That does not make any sense. Why would I want to give a discount to anyone?" Hedgehog asked.

"Because you've told yourself you have no other choice," said Fox. "In your mind, your biggest competitor—the Internet—is offering a discounted rate and you need to offer a discount to save the paper, right?"

"Well, yes, and Squirrel needs an answer right away, or the

advertisers might walk," Hedgehog protested. "Plus, Toad Sr. is threatening to shut down the paper."

"One of the clues that we might be acting like the wolf is that we don't gather much information before jumping to a conclusion," Fox explained.

Just then, Fieldmouse knocked on the door and entered carrying a tray with the coffee and muffins. Hedgehog waved him in.

"I brought blueberry bran and carrot muffins," Fieldmouse said, bringing in the tray and setting it down on the coffee table.

"Thanks, Fieldmouse," Hedgehog said, as Fieldmouse set out the sugar and soy milk.

Hedgehog continued, "I understand that it's ideal to gather as much information as possible, but what about decisions that must be made quickly? What if there is no time to gather evidence?"

"Sometimes you just have to make a decision immediately," Fox agreed. "If your car suddenly catches on fire, you have to pull over to the side of the road and jump out. But that is not how the best decisions tend to be made."

"So hasty decisions are always wrong?" Hedgehog clarified.

"Decisions that have not been well thought-out are often wrong," said Fox.

"I'm really sorry to listen in, but I can't help myself," said Fieldmouse, who had just finished setting out the food. "I read a lot about neuroscience and I thought that decisions made quickly were often correct because the intuitive brain is smarter than the rational brain."

"He also reads books about string theory," said Hedgehog.

Fox smiled. "Well, aren't you full of surprises. You are absolutely correct. When you are making a complex decision—a decision where a lot of data might overwhelm the rational brain and the emotional brain is more effective—that quick, intuitive response can be a very powerful tool. But it is neither a failsafe approach nor effective for every type of decision. It works best when you have already put in the time to develop expertise in an area. Then your response can be trusted. It's why doctors and others who have to make quick decisions receive so much training. The main problem with the snap decision in a business setting is that, even if it is the right decision, it is hard to gain commitment from others since they cannot see how you arrived at your recommendation. Lots of good decisions fail in the implementation stage because nobody felt committed."

"Makes sense, thank you," said Fieldmouse, excusing himself from the room.

"Smart guy," said Fox.

Hedgehog nodded, "I really don't know much about him, I'm afraid."

Hedgehog took a sip of his coffee and sighed deeply. "So you think that I should not extend the discount?" Hedgehog asked.

"I haven't a clue," said Fox. "But by the time your management meeting rolls around this afternoon, you'll have a framework for making these decisions."

"Okay," Hedgehog said, hoping Fox was right. "So, what have you learned so far?" Fox asked.

"I should have become a dentist like my mother wanted me to be," Hedgehog said.

"What have you really learned?" Fox asked.

"I need to gather information before making decisions, surround myself with squirrels," Hedgehog said, "and avoid the wolf."

"Exactly. You're ready for step two."

# CHAPTER FIVE

# ENGAGE THE FOX: GENERATING IDEAS

## Critical Thinking Process

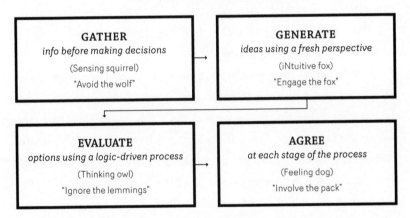

**GATHER**
*info before making decisions*
(Sensing squirrel)
"Avoid the wolf"

**GENERATE**
*ideas using a fresh perspective*
(iNtuitive fox)
"Engage the fox"

**EVALUATE**
*options using a logic-driven process*
(Thinking owl)
"Ignore the lemmings"

**AGREE**
*at each stage of the process*
(Feeling dog)
"Involve the pack"

"Let's review. MBTI measures the two different ways creatures tend to figure out what is happening. The first way is to use their senses to gather information about what is happening. The second step is to generate ideas about what might be going on."

**GENERATE**
*ideas using a fresh perspective*
(iNtuitive fox)
"Engage the fox"

"So intuitive is the opposite of sensing?" Hedgehog asked.

"In a way, yes, although both are key parts of the thinking process. Intuitive creatures are less interested in facts and details and more interested in patterns and relationships and in the big picture. Rather than trying to identify an issue or problem, they try to figure out the cause of the problem. Since my clients often hire me to bring a fresh perspective to the table and help them generate ideas, and foxes are generally known for their wily nature, I use the fox as a memory helper."

"Foxes are known for their ability to come up with new ideas," Hedgehog said, remembering his interviews with Desert Fox.

Fox nodded. "When I was a little kit, my grandpa used to tell me stories about hunting in the days before the treaty."

"This story doesn't involve hunting hedgehogs, does it?" Hedgehog said squeamishly.

Fox smiled and shook his head. "Nope. Just chickens."

"Carry on," Hedgehog said.

"Well, before my grandfather opened a chain of vegan sandwich shops, he was a famous chicken thief. I asked him one time what it was that made him so successful. As a fox, he was not the largest or the fastest creature out there and if he wanted to eat, he had to be more strategic. Instead of thinking of the usual places to find food, such as down by the duck pond, he wandered into the closest human town and found a chicken coop. Most creatures avoided towns inhabited by people because of their guns and their traps, but my grandfather noticed that each night, after supper, a particular chicken farmer used to drift off to sleep while listening to the radio. Grandpa would watch the chicken coop from the woods until he saw the farmer sit down in his easy chair and switch on the radio. Then he'd make his move. He'd never take more than one chicken; there was no point in being greedy and blowing his cover. By taking the time to generate some creative ways to hunt, he was able to feed his family well in spite of his small size."

"Are you telling me that I'm going to have to start stealing chickens?" Hedgehog asked.

"Not at all," chuckled Fox. "And believe me, he's atoned for each chicken he ate. But I am saying that, for you, gathering information is probably going to feel more comfortable than generating new ideas."

"So if we have to generate new ideas in order to save the paper, I'm doomed," Hedgehog said glumly.

"Don't confuse preference with destiny," Fox said. "Most investigative journalists are intuitive types interested in exploring relationships and connections and cause. But you won a Mewlitzer Prize for your interviews with Desert Fox. I read those articles because Desert Fox is my second cousin, once removed. Your article was great because you chased down every detail and because you described everything you saw and heard. It was like I was there. But I bet that job caused you to work outside your comfort zone a lot, which is why you switched into administration."

"So because I'm not a fox, I have to engage one?" Hedgehog asked. "Are you telling me that every time I want to make a decision, I need to hire you?"

"I'd love it if I could get away with that," Fox laughed. "But no. Have you ever heard of Archilochus?"

Hedgehog shook his head.

"He was a human Greek poet who lived around 650 BC. He wrote a line I've always kind of liked: 'The fox knows many things; the hedgehog one big thing.'" Fox said.

Hedgehog paused a moment. "Well, I don't like it at all," he said. "It makes it sound like I'm ignorant."

"Not at all," said the Fox. "Back in the days of the ancient Greeks, when animals used to eat each other, one of the few small animals a fox would not bother trying to attack was the hedgehog. You see, when you do your one big thing—you roll into a ball and stick out your 5,000 or so spines—you are almost impossible to eat."

"A fox killed my grandfather," Hedgehog said quietly.

"Oh, gosh, Hedgehog." Fox said. "I'm sorry about that. Gee, how awkward."

Hedgehog nodded. It wasn't personal. Animals killed each other all the time before the peace treaty was signed. During a heated disagreement, Toad Sr. had once pointed out that his great-great-aunt had been eaten by a hedgehog.

Fox was respectfully quiet for a moment before continuing.

"Hedgehogs make great business leaders. Lots of companies become successful by doing one thing really well," Fox explained.

Hedgehog nodded. "Like Crabapple makes beautiful technology devices. Or Nestflicks has mastered streaming. Or Mole-Mart manages the supply chain?"

Fox nodded, "Exactly. Hedgehog-like thinking is really, really important when it comes to defining who you are and making really good products. You don't want to be all things to all creatures. It's also very important in the implementation stage of the thinking process."

"So why didn't you write down 'engage the hedgehog'?" Hedgehog asked.

"Great question," Fox said. "When it comes to thinking critically, Hedgehogs can draw from a wealth of information. They can be really good at making those quick decisions based on a lifetime of accumulated expertise in one area. It goes back to the coffee question. If I ask you if you want a coffee, you know the answer. You know that, by coffee, I mean a beverage that is hot and tasty and contains caffeine. If I asked a toddler if she wants a coffee, she'd have no idea what to answer. She has no experience base."

Hedgehog nodded.

Fox continued, "When you are dealing with new issues during times of rapid change, you become the toddler. Your experience no longer helps you because the world has changed. Sometimes, all of that expertise can even be a disadvantage. You want to stick with what's always worked. Let's say I change the concept of coffee. Now it's cold and tastes terrible and makes you tired. That toddler might have an advantage when I ask her if she wants a coffee. She'll ask what it is and will say no. You'd say yes, drawing on your previous experience, and would be in for an ugly surprise. Sometimes it's useful to have someone who has a fresh perspective: someone who can observe the situation and ask a lot of questions. Like when you say, 'Customers are taking their business to the Internet,' I would be willing to bet that everyone in the newspaper business would agree. There are stats showing that your readership is falling and that online readership is increasing. There are stats showing your ad revenue is down and other stats showing online revenue is up. You see correlation and you see cause. All I'm asking is, how do you know that it's true?"

"I've heard it from customers," Hedgehog said.

"Have you heard this directly from all of your customers?" Fox asked.

Hedgehog shook his head. While it was true that he knew a lot about newspapers—how they run and how a good story is put together—he did not have in-depth knowledge of *The Gazette's* readers or advertisers. He knew about Raccoon from Toad Sr. and Squirrel. He knew about Big Bear and Turtle from Squirrel and Magpie from Squirrel and Badger. He'd just assumed he understood the advertising issue, but maybe that wasn't the case. He certainly did not want to be making important decisions based on wrong information. Maybe there was something to what Fox was saying.

"One of the major pitfalls with the idea generation part of the thinking process is that you don't generate enough ideas. Foxes tend to bring a new perspective to the table. Had my grandfather assumed that wild birds were the only source of food, he would have starved to death. He needed to generate some new ideas. The proverbial foxes will throw ideas out there that may seem wacky but will get you to think about the issue in another way. This can be very useful."

"This is like your grandfather realizing he no longer has to steal chickens?" Hedgehog added somewhat facetiously.

"Of course," Fox laughed. "Before you think that you have to slash ad prices and then cut all of your costs by an offsetting amount, consider that maybe this is not the case. Perhaps you can generate some other ideas. Don't let the urgency of Raccoon's request or the stress of Toad Sr.'s threat to shutter the paper force you down a certain path. Take the time to step back and assess what is really going on."

"But even if Raccoon had not asked for a discount, the newspaper business is going through tough times. Real or imagined, social media is competition. We have to get cheaper," Hedgehog said. "Raccoon did us a favor by making us focus on this now."

"I know that's what you think. And you may be right. My job, as the fox who knows many things, is to challenge your hedgehog expertise. We need to question your assumptions and put more options on the table. You believe that social media is killing newspapers and the only solution is to act more like the Internet. You've found lots of evidence to support this, but I'm challenging you to see if this is actually true or if you've simply found evidence supporting a false belief. "

"So, in other words, I'm going to need to put you on retainer. We don't employ any other foxes at the paper," Hedgehog said flatly.

Fox smiled. "That's the beauty of what I'm going to teach you," he said. "Just as you don't have to be a squirrel to think like a squirrel, you don't have to be a fox to think like one."

"My head hurts," Hedgehog said. He only had until the end of the day to decide on the advertising strategy, if he'd accept Rabbit's resignation, and if he'd have to cut costs. He really did not have time to change the way he thought. "I'm a senser. I'm not intuitive. Does that mean I'll never be a fox?"

"Nope. Again, these are just preferences. Just as you can sign your name with your left paw, you can also use nonpreferential thinking styles. Remember, you won a Mewlitzer Prize for your interview with Desert Fox. You were the first journalist to figure out how important he was in brokering the peace treaty. You were able to be intuitive when you needed to be and then used your sensing preferences to do the detailed research that distinguished you in the field. But the good news is that you do not run this paper by yourself. You will have lots of intuitive types on board who love to generate new ideas. Can you think of any idea guys here?"

"Rabbit is amazing," Hedgehog confirmed. "I don't think the word *no* is in her vocabulary. If one lead on a story dries up, she gets her reporters to start pursuing another angle. She always knows what readers want to read."

"Sounds like a fox to me," said Fox.

"But we might lose her to the competition," Hedgehog said despairingly.

"Who else likes big ideas?" Fox pressed.

Hedgehog thought for a minute. "Toad Jr. is definitely intuitive. He comes up with lots of ideas—but most of them are crazy."

"Intuitive types often do come up with crazy ideas," Fox said. "Remember, they are not interested in grounding them in reality the way sensers are. Of the ten ideas they might generate, nine may be crazy. But that's okay, because you only need one good idea. Besides, what seems crazy now might not be crazy in the future. As a kid, did you ever think you'd be able to run your entire life from a pocket-sized phone? Face it, right now you believe that your only two options are to lower ad rates and cut head count, or cede your business to the Internet. In either scenario, Toad Sr. will probably shut you down. A crazy idea is what you need."

"Okay, so let's assume we've generated ten crazy ideas, now what do we do?" Hedgehog asked flatly.

"As a thinker, you're going to like the next step," Fox said.

# CHAPTER SIX

# INVITE THE OWL: EVALUATING IDEAS

### Critical Thinking Process

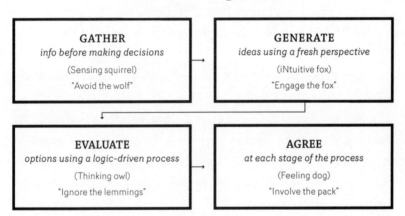

"So Sensing and Intuition describe the two ways most creatures prefer to gather information. There are also two distinct ways creatures like to process the information they have: Thinking and Feeling. The T in your ISTJ profile stands for thinking, which is the third step in the critical thinking process," Fox said.

**EVALUATE**
*options using a logic-driven process*
(Thinking owl)
"Ignore the lemmings"

"I have a preference for thinking," Hedgehog said. "So what does that mean?"

"Thinkers, like you, are very analytical and prefer to use logic to reach decisions," Fox explained. "You might find yourself making lists of pros and cons or assigning weights to various factors. Business schools spend a lot of time helping build thinking skills. Most organizations are pretty good at this step, especially when it's business as usual."

"But there is still a pitfall, I imagine," Hedgehog said. "Something about lemmings?"

"Have you ever talked to a lemming?" Fox asked.

Hedgehog thought a moment. When he was a reporter he'd talked to many species: elephants, lions, snakes, monkeys, and whales. But he was pretty sure he'd never spoken directly with a lemming.

"You know, I don't think I have," he said.

"Well," said Fox, "it's not surprising. There are not a lot of them around anymore."

"Aren't they the ones who jump off cliffs en masse?" Hedgehog asked.

"Sort of," Fox said. "Right after the peace treaty was signed, the lemming population became very overcrowded. A large group of them decided to migrate overseas. Lemmings are good swimmers, but they grossly underestimated the size of the sea. Most of them did not make it to the other side."

"Gosh, that's really sad," Hedgehog said.

"When you are looking over a chasm in business, there will always be creatures telling you that you can make it and urging you to jump. Often they say things like 'We must do this!'" Fox explained. "Remember, it's easy to jump on the bandwagon until you realize the bandwagon is headed over a cliff. Had just one of those lemmings publicly asked, 'Hey, how many miles across is this sea? Have any of us gone that distance? How cold is the water? Is there any food out there?' the crisis might have been averted."

"Those lemmings needed a fox," Hedgehog said.

"What they needed was an owl," Fox replied. "Owls—those with a preference for thinking—love to sit up high and analyze what is going on to make sure that they are not headed toward a cliff when everyone starts running.

"Well, that sounds like Owl, our finance director. Her financial analysis is always very sound. Just when I think she could not possibly analyze the numbers any more, she sends me another scenario. She likes to present me with pros and cons and tends to weigh the information. That's why she's the perfect finance director. She presents me information the way I'd like to receive it."

Fox nodded. "One of the beautiful things about understanding the personality types of your team is that you can tailor the presentation of information to appeal to their natural preferences. Are there any other owls on your team? Besides you?"

Hedgehog thought for a moment. "Toad Jr. in promotions seems like he is logical, even though I hate to give him credit for thinking," Hedgehog said. "Rabbit, our editor, is definitely a thinker. In fact, whenever she saw that creatures were running off to do something without thinking it through, she'd refer to them as lemmings. She thinks this whole social media thing is leading the industry right off a cliff," Hedgehog said.

"So even though you have a preference for thinking, it's great that you have colleagues who will evaluating ideas, too. It is critical given that you have so many decisions on the table right now," Fox said.

Hedgehog nodded.

"After this, there is one final step," Fox said.

"I don't think I'm going to like this one," Hedgehog said.

# CHAPTER SEVEN

# INVOLVE THE PACK: SEEKING AGREEMENT

## Critical Thinking Process

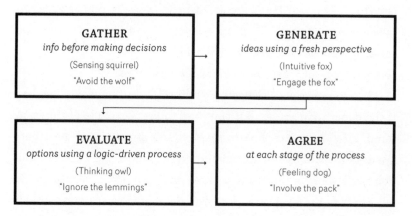

| GATHER | GENERATE |
|---|---|
| *info before making decisions* | *ideas using a fresh perspective* |
| (Sensing squirrel) | (Intuitive fox) |
| "Avoid the wolf" | "Engage the fox" |

| EVALUATE | AGREE |
|---|---|
| *options using a logic-driven process* | *at each stage of the process* |
| (Thinking owl) | (Feeling dog) |
| "Ignore the lemmings" | "Involve the pack" |

"The opposite preference to Thinking is Feeling," Fox continued. "Feeling types tend to view an issue with their personal values system in mind. Thinking types often pride themselves on keeping their feelings and personal biases out of the decision-making process. Feeling types believe that a good decision cannot be made in isolation and think that understanding how stakeholders will accept a decision is key. This brings us to the fourth and final step in critical thinking: Agree."

```
┌─────────────────────────────────┐
│              AGREE              │
│   at each stage of the process  │
│          (Feeling dog)          │
│         "Involve the pack"      │
└─────────────────────────────────┘
```

"I know these guys," Hedgehog said. "In meetings, they are always saying, "We need to consider how others are going to feel about this.""

"It sounds like you have some feeling types on your team," Fox observed.

"Well, I was actually thinking of Dog. She manages AR. She's a former champion French bulldog who has a business degree. She's been at *The Gazette* longer than I and was the first domesticated animal the paper hired. When I mentioned the notion of cost-cutting, she immediately warned me of the impact on morale. In a situation like this, where our backs are against the wall, I'm not sure we can take feelings into consideration. I mean, if I can't figure this out, we could lose our advertisers, Toad Sr. will shut down the paper, and we could all lose our jobs. Then we'd all feel really bad!"

Fox contemplated Hedgehog's point. "True, you would feel bad if the paper went under. But you need to keep a couple of things in mind. First, no matter how brilliant your idea may be, if the others are not on board to execute it, your idea will most likely fail. Second, don't sell animals short. I've worked with companies facing layoffs where creatures have voted for wage rollbacks rather than see their friends lose their jobs and take on the stress of a heavier workload. Never underestimate the power of engaged employees," Fox said.

"Well, given that I'm an introverted thinker and don't have any feelings at all, I suppose that having feeling types like Dog around reminds me to think about the staff," Hedgehog joked.

Fox smiled. "First of all, just because something is not your natural preference, it does not mean you cannot learn to be good at it. Your profile is ISTJ. You don't naturally look at the creatures' side of things. And yet, you are CEO of a newspaper. Clearly you are highly skilled at relating to others. But the good thing is, you do not have to do this alone. I bet your organization is filled with managers who push you to think about the impact of decisions on others."

"Unfortunately," joked Hedgehog.

"Feeling types may annoy you, but they are a key part of the thinking process," Fox said gently. "The more creatures who are involved in the thinking process, the better."

"Have you ever met a camel?" Hedgehog asked.

Fox paused a moment, thinking of all of the animals he'd met over the years. "Um, no, I don't believe I've met a camel," Fox said, puzzled.

"Odd creatures. Lumpy and strange. The best description of them I ever heard was 'a camel is a horse designed by a committee,'" Hedgehog said.

Fox chuckled, "Not a fan of teams?"

"My MBTI indicates I'm an I," Hedgehog said dryly. "Remember, there is no I in Team."

"Har har," Fox said, smiling. "Have you ever heard of a human named Victor Vroom?"

Hedgehog shook his head.

"Vroom, a professor at Yale School of Management—a prestigious human school much like Vale University—wrote a terrific book called *Leadership and Decision Making*. In it, he noted that a significant number of projects did not achieve the desired results. Vroom studied the decision-making process used for decisions that failed and those that succeeded. Would you like to know what he discovered?" Fox asked.

"Of course!" Hedgehog said.

"First, success came from choosing the best possible solution. That speaks to gathering all of the information required, generating a number of possible solutions, and evaluating those solutions. Often things fail not because people selected the wrong solution, but rather because the right solution was never even considered."

"Okay," Hedgehog said cautiously.

"The second thing that was required in order to increase the odds of success was that the team had to be committed to implementing that solution. The best idea on the planet will not lead to successful results if nobody has made the commitment to implement it," Fox explained. "A key reason why animals make poor decisions is that they do not involve the right players in the process. Key stakeholders will make sure that all of the issues are considered before a decision is made. They can be very helpful with the gathering of information and generation and evaluation of ideas. Moreover, since they were involved in the thinking process, stakeholders are more likely to agree with whatever decision is made. Involvement builds commitment and commitment brings success. Vroom discovered that by making better decisions and gaining more buy-in, you will greatly increase your chance of a successful outcome."

"What's the difference between involvement and commitment?" Hedgehog asked.

"Anyone who shows up for the meeting is involved," Fox clarified. "Commitment means you have a stake in the process and the results. There used to be an old joke about the difference between the two. Have you ever heard of bacon and eggs?"

"Yes," said Hedgehog, wrinkling his nose.

"Well, when you think about bacon and eggs, the chicken is involved and the pig is committed. He has skin in the game, so to speak."

"Thanks for clarifying, I think," said Hedgehog feeling slightly nauseous. "I just worry that as an introvert and a thinker, I'm kind of doomed here. How can I get buy-in?"

"Everyone has natural strengths that can contribute to the critical thinking process," said Fox. "The key is to know where you are strong, and then rely on your team members to help you in areas where you are not as comfortable. Dog is a born feeler. Rely on her to bring that aspect to the table."

"So are you saying that, for any decision, I have to solicit the opinions of the entire company? We'll never get anything done!"

Fox shook his head. "Many decisions can be made on your own. Like whether you want a coffee. But if it's a big decision, and the stakes are high if you fail, it's smart to engage others—squirrels, foxes, owls and dogs—to get better decisions and more buy-in."

"So what's the pitfall in this step?" asked Hedgehog.

"Skipping it," said Fox. "In many ways, involving the pack is probably the most important step. By involving everyone from the outset, there won't be any big surprises at this stage. Colleagues can't question your decisions if they were involved from the beginning. Do you see the value of seeking agreement along the way?"

"I do. It's not my natural tendency, though. If I think I know a good solution, I'm not sure why everyone else can't see it and simply get on board. It's frustrating. I'll really need to rely on creatures like Dog to help me," Hedgehog admitted.

"Is there anyone else besides Dog?" Fox asked.

Hedgehog thought a moment. "Deer, our circulation director, is amazing. She fights to keep the TV schedule in the paper. Even though everyone keeps telling us the guide is obsolete, there are still customers, particularly older ones, who plan their week according to its TV listings. Since Deer's circulation team fields the calls from readers whenever the schedule is missing from their Saturday paper, she is passionate about this."

"Team members with a preference for feeling will help you iden-tify stakeholders you had not normally considered. They will also help keep in mind other value-based issues such as the impact of a decision on the environment." Fox said.

"My assistant, Fieldmouse, is constantly bringing things like that to my attention," Hedgehog said.

"Sounds like you are surrounded by animals with a preference for feeling. If you let them help you, involving the pack should be easy. Okay, so let's review," Fox said, pointing at the card.

## Critical Thinking Process

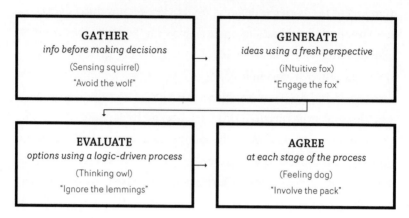

"The card outlines the basic process for critical thinking. It should help you remember what we have talked about so far today. Does it all make sense?" Fox asked.

"It does," Hedgehog said. "It will remind me what steps I need to take, let me know what preference I need to be using at each point in the decision-making process, indicate who might be able to help me, and remind me of the pitfalls to avoid. I think I'm normally pretty good at avoiding the wolf since my background as a reporter makes me ask a lot of questions. I'm not as good at seeing other possibilities, so I need to engage the fox. I don't think I am tempted to rush off a cliff, so ignoring the lemmings is easy. But I tend not to get other creatures on board as much as I should, so I need to involve the pack. I think I have a good grip on how the intuitive/sensing and thinking/feeling preferences impact my thinking. As an ISTJ, does the I or the J come into play at some point in this process?"

"Great question," said Fox. "A sensing or intuitive preference tells you how you prefer to acquire information. Do you gather facts and data or generate patterns and relationships? Thinking or feeling speaks to how you process information: whether you take an analytical approach or prefer to consider how others might react to the outcome. These are the main components of the thinking process. But understanding the other preferences—introversion/extraversion and judging/perceiving can help you avoid some of the common thinking pitfalls."

"Like what?' Hedgehog asked.

"Well," said Fox, "extraverts tend to feel very comfortable expressing their ideas to the outside world. There is a danger that their ideas can dominate meetings. That's why, when you do activities like brainstorming to generate ideas, you must make sure that everyone in the room has a chance to speak up. Extraverts like to speak out and may not wait until their ideas are well formulated. Introverts are more likely to keep good ideas private, mulling them over a bit more before they share them with the group."

"That sounds like me," Hedgehog said. "I like things to be perfect before I share."

"The judging and perceiving preferences indicate whether, when dealing with the outside world, you prefer to acquire information (through sensing/intuition) or assess the information (through thinking/feeling). Judging types like to have matters settled and want to assess the information to reach a decision. Sometimes they will rush through the information-gathering process because they'd like finality. They can miss finding some good solutions. Perceivers, on the other hand, would prefer to stay in the information-gathering phase indefinitely. It's true that with no time or resources constraints, everyone could find an optimal solution. This is, of course, not the reality of business or life. We are trying to find the best solution in a reasonable time frame. Perceivers often need to be encouraged to reach a decision."

"So that's another reason to have lots of creatures at the table—to get a balance of types," said Hedgehog.

"Exactly." Fox smiled.

"I like how there is a framework and how I can anticipate some of the pitfalls in advance," said Hedgehog.

"A framework often makes things easier. That way you won't freeze when the going gets tough."

Hedgehog nodded and looked at his watch. "It's already after noon and I'm starving," he said. "Let's go grab some lunch."

"Good idea," Fox said. "In times of crisis, we often skip meals and give up sleep, but one needs to be well fed and rested in order to make good decisions. Besides, if I get too hungry, your head of advertising might start to look awfully tasty."

Hedgehog chuckled nervously, hoping that Fox was joking. He told Fieldmouse that he'd be back shortly and took Fox down the hall to the cafeteria.

# CHAPTER EIGHT

# AN UNEXPECTED INTERRUPTION

Both Fox and Hedgehog were pleasantly full after a big lunch of fresh greens and roasted mushroom sandwiches from the company cafeteria.

Fox and Hedgehog walked back into Hedgehog's office and closed the door. They both sat down in the velvet club chairs.

"Can I ask you something?" Fox asked.

"Anything," Hedgehog said.

"Do you usually eat lunch at your desk?"

"Why do you ask?" Hedgehog said.

"The employees looked surprised to see you in the cafeteria," he said.

"Maybe they were surprised to see me sitting there with a fox," Hedgehog said.

"Perhaps," Fox said.

"I usually eat lunch at my desk," Hedgehog admitted. "I guess it's the introvert in me. I just figure that no one wants to eat with the boss around. They might want to badmouth me or something and can't if I'm sitting there . . ."

"It's hard to involve the pack when you don't really mingle with them," Fox said gently.

Hedgehog felt a bit defensive. "I know. I guess that's one of the pitfalls we were discussing before lunch. I feel weird going into the cafeteria knowing that I might have to make a decision to downsize. Leaders have to make tough decisions, and it's hard to do that if you are worried about winning a popularity contest."

"Eliciting buy-in is different from winning a popularity contest," Fox said.

"So, are you saying that I should be asking my employees what to do about the paper?" Hedgehog asked.

They were interrupted by a knock at the door. It was Toad Jr.

"Can I talk to you for a moment?" he asked Hedgehog, completely ignoring Fox. "Alone."

Hedgehog looked at Fox. "Well, I'm in the middle of something right now; can it wait?"

"Not really," Toad Jr. said. "I'm pretty sure you are going to want to hear what I have to say."

"Well," Hedgehog said, "spit it out, then. I haven't got all day . . . "

"I need to speak to just you," he said, glaring at Fox.

Fox interrupted. "Please, you two go ahead. I have to do a couple of things to set up for the meeting. Where is the boardroom?"

Hedgehog pointed to the boardroom down the hall.

"I'll be in there," Fox said and gave Toad Jr. a toothy grin as he exited Hedgehog's office.

Hedgehog turned to Toad Jr. "What's up?" he said, not masking the annoyance in his voice. "I was in an important meeting."

"What are you doing hanging out with a criminal?" Toad Jr. asked.

"What are you talking about?" asked Hedgehog.

"That guy you were with in the cafeteria. Fox. He was a chicken thief in college," Toad Jr. said.

"What are you talking about?" Hedgehog asked with exasperation.

"I was sitting with Lynx, one of our reporters, in the cafeteria when the two of you walked in," Toad Jr. began. "Lynx asked what you were doing with Tad 'The Brain' Fox. The guy is a hardened criminal. Did you notice the gold pin on his jacket lapel? Like an egg? He stole it from the chickens and wears it as a trophy."

Hedgehog felt ill. Lynx was the paper's crime reporter and tended to get his facts right. He had noticed Fox's egg pin. Fox said his grandfather was a chicken thief and he seemed to make a lot of jokes about eating other animals. Perhaps Lynx was right.

"He's a chicken thief? But that's highly illegal!" Hedgehog said with astonishment. When he'd hired Fox, he was simply so grateful to have someone willing to help him make some very hard decisions that he never bothered to ask any questions. There's no way he'd knowingly hire a chicken thief to help sort out his newspaper business. If Toad Sr. found out about this, he'd be fired on the spot.

Toad Jr. continued, "Lynx went to college with him on the other side of the mountain. They were a little behind the rest of us socially and theirs was the first generation of animals to grow up post-treaty in their area. There was still a lot of animosity between the animals who'd formerly been predators and prey. The chickens had been experiencing a number of break-ins in their fraternity house and the foxes were the most likely culprits. Fox ran the fox fraternity at the time. The chickens asked campus security—mostly hounds, with their noses for trouble—to look into the matter. The security hounds picked up Tony 'Muscles' Fox and Shirley 'Lightning' Fox and loaded them into the security van for questioning. As they were driving them through a wooded area near the campus, the two foxes broke free and ran into the woods. The hounds gave chase. Unbeknownst to them, Tad 'The Brain' Fox had jumped onto the back of the van and hung onto the door handle. He must have let Muscles and Lightning out when the van stopped for some reason and the three outlaws escaped into the woods."

Hedgehog's eyes were wide with disbelief. "Then what happened?"

Toad Jr. happily continued. He was in his element when he had a nice piece of gossip to spread. It's why entertainment blogging was a natural fit for him. "Well, the hounds, seeing the foxes escape from the van, started to chase them through the woods. Somehow Tad Fox—your lunchtime companion—managed to double back to the van, start it up, and drive it to a roadside chip van with a reputation for selling illegal meat. He got his paws on some contraband meat sausages—I'm sure he ate them all the time when he thought nobody was looking—and went back to the woods to set a trap. The hounds, still chasing the outlaws, smelled the illegal meat. Being law-abiding citizens, they, of course, felt compelled to investigate. They stopped chasing the foxes and started running towards the scent of cooked meat. Fox lured them into the back of their own van, closed the door behind them, and then kidnapped them."

Hedgehog was flabbergasted. These were serious allegations. "Did he have to go to jail?" he asked.

"Nope." Toad Jr. shook his head. "He probably paid somebody off. Still, it makes me uncomfortable to have him in our midst."

"I need to get him out of here," Hedgehog said, his brow in a cold sweat. How could he have been so foolish as to hire a known criminal?

"Look," Toad Jr. said, "Nobody needs to know about this except you, me, and Lynx. Just get rid of the guy."

Toad Jr. left the meeting room and Hedgehog followed him into the hall. His head was spinning. Had he just hired a criminal to help him?

Fox stuck his head out the boardroom door. "Everything okay?"

Hedgehog went into the boardroom and closed the door. "No, everything is not okay," he hissed. He was trying to whisper so that nobody who happened to be passing in the hallway might hear. "Toad Jr. just informed me that you are a chicken thief and a hound kidnapper."

Fox shook his head sadly.

"That story never goes away," he said. "Let me guess, you were told the story by a hound?"

"I need you to leave the building immediately," Hedgehog said. "Or I'll call security. We have two grizzly bears here on staff. I would go quietly if I were you."

"Look, I'll go, but for what it's worth, I want to tell you what really happened that day," Fox said resignedly.

"Why should it matter to me?" Hedgehog asked.

"Because it has a lot to do with what we covered this morning," Fox said.

"You have two minutes," Hedgehog said, sitting in one of the swivel chairs around the large oak boardroom table.

"Okay," Fox began, "I went to university on the other side of the mountain. The campus was beautiful: I chose it for its proximity to the woods, since hiking is one of my favorite things to do. The local town was a bit backward, however, which was a real surprise. I had gone to boarding school with lots of other animals—my roommate and best friend was a mouse. We had all been born after the treaty was signed to end the barbaric practice of animals eating other animals. I may joke about it from time to time. It's a coping mechanism I use to help offset my distaste for the destruction my ancestors must have caused. Anyhow, at this university, foxes tended to hang out with their own species.  In time, I adjusted and even became president of the fox fraternity. One of my goals, as president, was to increase interspecies activity in the name of peace. I'd received a call from the head of the chicken fraternity that morning. Chicken House and Fox House collaborated on a number of philanthropic efforts and Gus Chicken and I were good friends. They'd had some things stolen— laptops and the like—and had asked campus security to look into it. One of the freshman chickens had been studying in her room with the window open when she overheard two hound security guards talking outside. They said that they were going to try to pin the theft on the foxes so that they could justify a good old-fashioned fox hunt in the woods. "

Fox's voice caught as he remembered the events of the past. "I know it's been two minutes. Should I go?" he asked Hedgehog.

Hedgehog shook his head. He wanted to hear the rest of the story. Fox poured himself a glass of ice water from the pitcher that had been placed in the boardroom by Fieldmouse in anticipation of their afternoon meeting.

Fox continued. "I was about to call an all-fox meeting when three hounds burst through the door and grabbed Tony and Shirley."

"Don't you mean Muscles and Lightning?" Hedgehog asked.

Fox shook his head. "Muscles and Lightning . . . oh how Tony would get a chuckle out of that. I love how the story always changes in the telling. Tony's frat nickname was 'Cakes' because he loved to eat sweets. He was the very opposite of muscles. Shirley's sorority sisters called her 'Beaker' because she was majoring in chemistry. She was a lovely vixen, but a snail could beat her in a footrace. I suppose the hounds did not want to admit to being bested by Cakes and Beaker. Muscles and Lightning make for a better story."

"Were you The Brain?" Hedgehog asked.

Fox shrugged, looking a bit embarrassed. "Yup, that detail did not change. So, the hound security guards threw Cakes and Beaker in the back of the van. Being young and foolish, I decided to jump onto the back of the van and hang on just as they were pulling away. When they got to the woods, they stopped the van. I jumped off and hid beneath the vehicle. They opened the doors to the back and told Cakes and Beaker that they'd have until the count of ten to run as fast and as far away as they could before the dogs gave pursuit. We'd all read about fox hunts in history class and I'm sure Cakes and Beaker were terrified."

Hedgehog's eyes were wide with amazement. "Go on," he urged Fox.

"Just then, a hound's phone rang and he picked it up to answer. As he was walking around talking loudly on the phone, I let out a low whistle from my hiding place beneath the van to attract the attention of Beaker, who was standing close to me. I whispered to Beaker that she and Cakes were to run as fast as possible until they heard a horn honking. They were to stop where they were, count to ten, and then run back toward the sound of the horn. They were to jump into the passenger side of the van and close and lock the doors."

"The van?" asked Hedgehog.

"I had noticed that one of the hounds had dropped the keys to the van on the ground as he fumbled to answer his phone. I had also noticed that about a mile back on the road, we'd passed a chip truck that had a funny smell. I had the beginnings of a plan in my head. Anyway, the hound hung up from his call and loudly started counting to ten. Cakes and Beaker started running. On the count of seven, the hounds took off after them, snarling and growling. As soon as they were out of sight, I started up the van and sped back to the chip truck I'd seen on the way there. I asked the rough-looking pitbull behind the counter for some sausage."

"Meat sausage?" Hedgehog asked in horror. "That's illegal."

"I know," said Fox, "but I figured that any guys setting up a fox hunt were not too interested in the law and would likely be enticed by the scent of meat. The chip truck owner looked me over to see if I was some sort of police officer or official, and then he took the pile of twenty dollar bills I'd put on the counter—money I'd had on me to put a deposit on some kegs for the homecoming game. He handed me a big bag of greasy sausage, and barked, 'If anybody asks, it's roadkill.'"

"Horrible!" Hedgehog cringed.

Fox continued, "I sped back to the clearing in the woods where I'd left everyone, hoping I was not too late. I threw open the doors on the back of the van and lowered the loading ramp. I left the passenger door open for Cakes and Beaker. I spread out the sausages at the top of the ramp and all over the back of the van. I blasted the horn ten or twelve times and then hid underneath the ramp."

"What happened?" Hedgehog asked breathlessly.

"I heard the sounds of a creature crashing through the under-brush and the hound who'd been driving came running on all fours towards the van. On all *fours*! That's how primitive the hunt had made him. He ran up the ramp, grabbing up several sausages in his mouth. Then his colleagues followed and when they were safely inside, I pushed up the ramp with all my might, blocking them in the back of the van. I slammed the doors and stuck a shovel I'd found in the back of the van through the handles to securely lock them in. Then Cakes and Beaker came tearing out of the forest. They jumped into the passenger side and I jumped into the driver's side behind the wheel. I hit the gas. All the way back to campus we could hear snarling and growling as the hounds tried to break through the metal barrier separating us from them. I pulled the van up in front of the police station and we jumped out. A couple of police bears took it from there."

Hedgehog was astounded. "So what happened then?"

"Well, we got back to campus and the police got a warrant to search the campus security office and found not only a big supply of illegal meat and betting forms for fox hunts, but also all of the chickens' laptops. I got my business degree paid for by an anonymous benefactor who read about my story in the local paper and I became an honorary member of the chicken fraternity."

"Is that why you wear an egg pin?" Hedgehog asked.

Fox pointed to a pin on his lapel, "It's the Golden Egg pin," he said. He unclipped it and handed it to Hedgehog to inspect. "*To Thaddeus P. Fox, for his amazing courage*," it read.

Hedgehog handed him back the pin, "I'm mortified," he said. "How could I have believed Toad Jr.?"

Fox smiled. "Well, it's like we discussed this morning."

He pointed to a stack of cards like the one he'd given Hedgehog.

## Critical Thinking Process

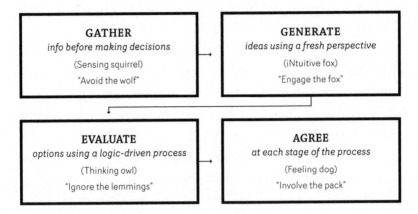

"Where were the holes in your thinking process?" Fox asked gently.

"I did not avoid the wolf," Hedgehog said, feeling ashamed. "I did not gather information before jumping to the conclusion that you were a thief. It seemed like things like your egg pin were evidence of wrongdoing when, in fact, they were evidence of your heroism."

"Don't feel too bad," Fox said. "You fell into a trap that allowed you to jump to a conclusion about me and then gather the evidence to support it."

"I feel so silly, having accused you like that," Hedgehog said.

"Don't," said Fox. "Look, you told me that your grandfather was eaten by a fox; you'll naturally be a bit nervous around me and think I just might be capable of doing something bad. So then Toad Jr., whom you know, tells you that he heard a story about a fox, whom you do not really know, and you believe him. He runs a gossip blog. He's the one who broke the story of starlet Maggie Muskrat's pregnancy, right? But then it turned out she had simply eaten a donut that day. Fact-checking is not his thing. A lot of the story he told you was true: just not the part about my character. Your conclusion was not a surprise. Remember, most creatures jump to a conclusion and then look for evidence to support their case."

Hedgehog looked at Fox, "You must think I'm really stupid. I mean, you tell me to watch out for this in the morning and by lunch I've already made this error."

Fox shook his head, "On the contrary," he said. "If you'd sent me home, then you'd have made a couple of classic mistakes. You'd have been like the wolf, making a decision before considering the evidence. You'd also have been following the lemmings. Toad Jr. and his source might have led you over a cliff before you had the opportunity to do some critical thinking about the issue."

"I'll say," said Hedgehog, shaking his head.

"But you obviously were listening, because you did one thing really well. Do you know what that was?" Fox asked.

Hedgehog shook his head.

"What is the first thing you did when you came in here?" Fox asked.

"I told you to get out because you were a bad guy," Hedgehog said glumly.

Fox shook his head. "Nope, if you'd have said that, I might have simply left. Like everyone else, foxes have self-doubts. I might have filled in the blanks for ways in which I'd failed you as a consultant. But instead you said, 'Toad Jr. just informed me that you are a chicken thief and a hound kidnapper.'"

Hedgehog blushed.

Fox continued, "Although I would have preferred it if you had phrased that as a question rather than as an accusation, you approached me in such a way that I was able to address your specific concerns and straighten things out."

"Oh," said Hedgehog. "So the key is to ask lots of questions."

"Yes!" Fox said brightly. "Asking lots of questions will help you know if you are dealing with wolves or lemmings. Questions will give you the evidence you need to support your decisions. If you have to make a snap decision, previous questions you asked should give you the background required to be able to make a good decision quickly."

"But you didn't have a lot of information when you had to plan how to help Cakes and Beaker," Hedgehog said.

"I had more information that you might think," Fox said. "Remember, I'd noticed the hound drop his keys when he fished his ringing phone out of his pocket. I'd seen the chip stand as we drove by, and, given the number of formerly carnivorous, criminal-looking types in the parking lot, and the funny smell, I guessed that they might sell contraband sausage there. I noticed the hounds chewing something constantly and I wondered if they might be chewing Chickorette gum. It's that gum they used to make that tasted a bit like chicken and is supposed to kill the craving for meat."

"And from all that you created your plan?" Hedgehog asked.

Fox nodded.

"Okay, I see how you gathered information, generated some ideas, and evaluated the information. But I don't see how you had buy-in. It's not like the hounds bought into being locked in the van," Hedgehog said.

"That's an excellent point," said Fox. "In my defense, I did have buy-in from the foxes and the chickens, and, later, the police bears, but you are right, the hounds were not on board. The best I could do was to neutralize them so that they did not sabotage my efforts. While it would be ideal if every decision were unanimously supported, that's just not realistic. It's against animal nature for everyone to agree all the time. What you can do by involving the pack is maximize buy-in. Not everybody will be happy with your decision, but hopefully they will feel heard and be able to understand why you took things in a different direction."

"The one thing that troubles me about this whole misunderstanding—other than simply the embarrassment of falsely accusing you of something, of course—is that I thought that Toad Jr. was supposed to be my go-to guy for helping me generate good ideas. He's a proverbial fox. And yet, he was the one taking things at face value and jumping to conclusions! He led me astray," Hedgehog said.

"Well," said Fox, "That's the tricky thing about this process. We are animals and we have natural biases that can get in the way of our thinking critically about a situation. In this case, Toad Jr. accepted gossip at face value and did not gather any information beyond that. Second, he did not evaluate the information. Like hedgehogs, toads fear foxes. You and Toad Jr. have an inherited bias to believe the worst about me. In this case you would need an intuitive fox-like thinker who did not share your fear of foxes. Is there anyone on staff who would not fear me instinctually?" Fox asked.

Hedgehog thought for a moment. "Dog, our AR manager. Foxes tend to be more scared of dogs than dogs of foxes, right?"

Fox nodded.

"Dog is great and, as one of our few domesticated employees, brings a fresh perspective to the table. Dog knows everybody because she does so much hiring. If I'd asked her, she could have called around to find out more about you," Hedgehog continued.

"Perfect. So in this case, Dog might have been your intuitive fox. Her fresh perspective that foxes are not scary would have allowed her to generate some different ideas about me."

"I see what you are saying," Hedgehog said. "But I'm a little confused. I thought that Dog was the feeler on my team."

"She is, and she is great at seeking consensus. That does not preclude her from also being an excellent contributor to other parts of the thinking process. These personality preferences do not mean that someone is definitively good or bad at any part of the thinking process. Toad Jr. is intuitive, but his inborn biases about the danger of foxes prevented him from being creative in his thinking. Every animal can contribute to every part of the thinking process. What my method shows is that in times of stress, we sometimes fail to think—period. By using a formal thinking process, we can make sure that we are drawing on our collective strengths and keeping our biases in check."

"It sounds like I should have Dog at the decision-making table a lot more than I do," Hedgehog said.

"I agree," said Fox. "If she's an intuitive feeler, a fox-dog, so to speak, she's a lovely counterbalance to your sensing and thinking squirrel-owl preferences. Given that you think so differently, however, it's not surprising that you might have undervalued her input in the past."

"I considered bringing her to the earlier meetings with Owl and Squirrel but she always seems to be on a different wavelength. I guess I could not see how she would be able to provide me answers about ad revenues or financial projections," Hedgehog confessed.

"Remember, it's not answers you are after at this point. If you get answers too early, you could be jumping to conclusions. Dog might not have answers, but she might ask some questions to help you reframe the issue." Fox said.

"I've undervalued her in the past, but I won't be making that same mistake again," said Hedgehog with determination in his voice. "I'll make sure I ask her opinion at our management meeting this afternoon."

"Involve the pack," said Fox.

Hedgehog looked at his watch. "I have twenty minutes before our meeting," he said. "I'd love you to be there. However, you will be seeing a lot of confidential numbers. I'd feel a lot better about the process if I could do a quick reference check," he said.

Fox smiled. "I think that you are really starting to understand what I've been saying. I know that time is tight, but asking the tough questions and doing the due diligence can save you so much trouble in the long run. I'll give you the phone number of the chicken who was president of his fraternity. He's now a senator. As well, I'll give you the number for the police chief at the time and for three of my consulting clients. And of course I'll sign a confidentiality agreement."

Hedgehog nodded, took the information, and headed back to his office to make the calls.

***

"Well?" asked Fox, as Hedgehog came back into the boardroom.

"Just like you said," Hedgehog replied. "The thing that I don't understand is why anyone would spread the other story."

"When animals decided that it made more sense to cooperate with one another, it represented a huge change for a lot of species. Change does not always bring out the best in folks. Animals get nervous. They fear for their place in society and financial security. They lash out at anyone they perceive to be against them. The rumor mill tends to speed up. It's not unlike what's going on in the newspaper business right now, no?"

Hedgehog nodded. "The chickens who work the printing presses keep threatening to strike. Maybe I can get that senator friend of yours to reason with them. Rabbit is threatening to quit. Our ad customers are ganging up on us. Our bank has threatened to pull our lines. And Toad Sr. has threatened to shut down the paper. I just feel like everyone is ganging up on me."

"Sounds like a tough situation," Fox said. "Any idea what might be helpful?"

"The government declaring online media to be illegal?" Hedgehog asked.

Fox laughed. "You might just find that the online world is a gift," he said.

There was a knock at the door. He looked up and saw that it was two o'clock. His management team was grouped around the board room door and they were all looking somewhat nervous.

"Involve the pack," Hedgehog said to Fox as he invited his senior management team to come into the boardroom and take a seat around the large oak table.

CHAPTER NINE

# FOX MEETS THE TEAM

"Thanks for joining me at such short notice," Hedgehog said to his team. "For those of you who have not met him, this is Fox. He's a management consultant who specializes in critical thinking. Given the importance of the decisions we are making today, I thought it made sense to bring in some outside help."

Toad Jr.'s mouth dropped open.

"Oh, yes," Hedgehog continued, looking at Toad Jr. "I just want to clarify one small matter. I just got off the phone with Senator Chicken and he told me that we have a true hero in our midst. In college, Fox was instrumental in bringing down a gang of hounds who were not upholding the peace treaty. We are lucky to have him with us today."

Toad Jr. blushed and made a note to talk to Lynx when the meeting was done. He did not like to look like a fool.

Fox walked around the boardroom table, shaking each animal's paw, hoof, or front foot. He spent an extra second or two shaking Toad Jr.'s front foot to show him that all had been forgiven. He then sat down at the table and took out his laptop to make some notes. He jotted down each animal's name and role in the company so he would not forget the cast of players:

*Squirrel—Advertising Director*
*Owl—Finance Director*
*Dog—Animal Resources Director*
*Fieldmouse—Executive Assistant to Hedgehog*
*Rabbit—Editor in Chief*
*Deer—Circulation Director*
*Badger—Production Director*
*Coyote—Information Technology Director*
*Toad Jr.—Promotions Director*

"Do you want to say a few words about yourself?" Hedgehog asked Fox.

"Sure," Fox said, clearing his throat. "My name is Thaddeus P. Fox. I specialize in helping organizations learn how to work through problems and identify opportunities more effectively. I'm here to observe your meeting and to guide you in thinking about the issues you face. I have signed a confidentiality agreement so I encourage you to speak freely."

The animals all nodded. Squirrel was a little nervous about the presence of a strange fox in the room but figured that he'd just have to get over it.

"Do you want to give them a quick run-down of the basic thinking process?" Hedgehog asked.

"Well, I don't want to dominate your meeting, but I'd be happy to give a quick overview. It might help to structure the meeting," Fox said. He pulled out some of his learning aid cards from the pile on the boardroom table and distributed them to the small group.

## Critical Thinking Process

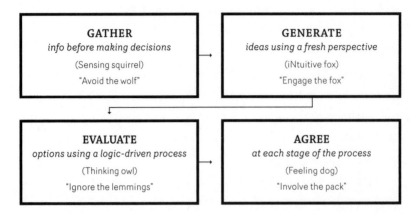

## Critical Thinking Skills for Issues Management

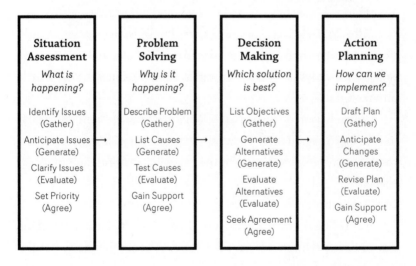

He gave the animals a few minutes to read over the card.

"Did you make these cards up just for us?" Squirrel asked. "You refer to a squirrel, a fox, an owl, and a dog."

Fox smiled. "Nope, but that worked out quite well, didn't it?" he said. "Thank heaven for stereotypes! Let me explain."

Fox took the group through a quick overview of how the basic thinking process worked. He taught them that by using the Good Geese Eat Apples approach, they would not miss any critical steps. He talked about how various animals brought different strengths and weaknesses to the table. Finally he talked about the pitfalls that can happen at each stage of the process and how this technique can help one avoid any missteps.

"It's a lot of information," Fox said. "I'm sure that questions will arise. The best way of really learning this material, however, is to apply it. You have a lot of important issues to discuss today and I'll turn things over to Hedgehog to continue. If I need to interject at any stage, I will."

He took his seat again, and Hedgehog thanked him.

"All right," Hedgehog said. "As you know, we have a lot of decisions to make right now. Raccoon, Bear, Magpie, and Turtle have asked for a decrease in their ad rates. Squirrel, can you talk a little bit about that?"

Squirrel cleared this throat. "Well, the four of them are clearly in cahoots. They all have the same request. They all want deep discounts on a go-forward basis or they all will be taking their business elsewhere."

"This is bad," said Hedgehog.

"Pause," said Fox, standing up. "Look, I don't want to interfere, but you are paying me for the privilege. We are jumping to conclusions here."

"I disagree," said Hedgehog. "Squirrel gathered information from the clients and discovered that they all want a discount. The alternatives generated are clear: give them a discount and keep the business or don't give them a discount and lose the business. Given that we need the business, we need to offer the discounts."

"I disagree," said Dog. "Maybe we don't need these four

advertisers at all. Lots of newspapers are lowering costs by putting more content online. Some are using paywalls to charge readers for the articles. They take ads from the better-paying national advertisers, as readership is no longer limited by geographical barriers."

Hedgehog was speechless. He did not know that Dog knew so much about the overall newspaper business.

"Anyhow," Dog continued, "I think that it is way too early in the process to make any decisions."

"We need to give the advertisers an answer by the end of the day," Squirrel said.

Deer, who ran circulation, looked at her watch. "We have four hours," she said. "I can get the paper delivered to the entire region in four hours. It's lots of time."

"I'd like to know now what our overall direction is going to be, said Rabbit. "I keep hearing online and digital media. But I have no interest in becoming some blog."

Toad Jr. jumped in. "You say *blog* like it's a dirty word! I'm not sure why everyone is so opposed to the idea of creating content that creatures want to read. My blog post about Maggie Muskrat's pregnancy had more readers in a week than this newspaper gets in a year."

"Which is fine, except she WASN'T PREGNANT!" Rabbit snapped.

The animals all started talking at once. Fox let out a loud whistle.

Everyone stopped talking and turned to look at him.

"Hello," Fox said, smiling. "Remember me?"

He pointed to the white board at the front of the boardroom. "May I?" he asked Hedgehog.

"Please," Hedgehog said.

Fox stood at the white board and picked up a marker. "Okay, so Hedgehog let me know a little about what was going on this morning. Let me put my memory to the test," he said.

He scribbled down some notes on the board, outlining the situation, as he had understood it from Hedgehog. He, of course, left out the part about potentially replacing Rabbit. That detail would reveal itself in due time.

> *Decide on Ad Discount*
>
> *Decide Ad Price Strategy*
>
> *Reduce Labor Costs and/or Shrink Paper*

"So, does everybody agree that this is what is going on?"

"No!" said Dog and Badger simultaneously.

"There is no way I can produce the paper with lower labor costs," Badger, who was in charge of production, said. "We are already stretched too thin. I thought we went over this at our last meeting."

"We need to move everything online," Toad Jr. said.

Rabbit let out an audible harrumph.

Badger was right. This was exactly like the last meeting, Hedgehog thought.

"So, it sounds like we are not in agreement, yet," Fox said. "Are we at the stage where we can make a decision about what to do?"

"We can choose between the rock and a hard place," said Rabbit. "I've heard no creative options."

"Does anyone else agree with Rabbit?" Fox asked.

A number of animals around the table nodded their heads.

"Do you feel that you know exactly what's going on in the business and need to have a brainstorming session to determine what options to pursue?" Fox asked.

There was silence in the room.

After a minute Hedgehog decided to speak. "You know, this may surprise all of you that I'm saying this, but after spending my entire life in this business and reading everything out there on what is happening to our industry, I'm not certain that I know what is going on, either broadly, or specifically, within our market. Things are moving so quickly and every paper seems to be scrambling to figure out their direction. Fox, as much as I hate to say this, given how pressed for time we are, I need to figure out exactly what is going on with our industry and our paper. Otherwise, we will just be making knee-jerk reactions to outside demands like those of our advertisers."

Fox smiled. "You have a courageous leader," he said to the group. "A lot of decisions, projects, and even companies fail because nobody will admit that things are changing quickly and you need some time to figure out what's going on."

Hedgehog appreciated the compliment, but he did not feel courageous. He felt overwhelmed and totally out of his comfort zone. He really should have become a dentist.

The management team was paying close attention. Owl and Squirrel appeared to be taking notes.

"It's time to formally look at the critical thinking skills you need to tackle a complex issue such as the one you are facing with your advertisers," Fox said. "Take a look at the back of the cards I distributed."

## Critical Thinking Skills for Issues Management

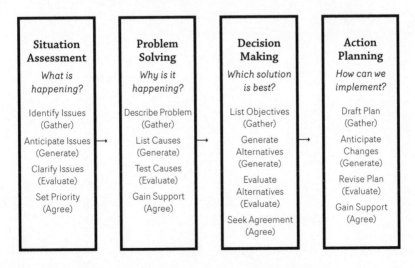

| Situation Assessment | Problem Solving | Decision Making | Action Planning |
|---|---|---|---|
| *What is happening?* | *Why is it happening?* | *Which solution is best?* | *How can we implement?* |
| Identify Issues (Gather) | Describe Problem (Gather) | List Objectives (Gather) | Draft Plan (Gather) |
| Anticipate Issues (Generate) | List Causes (Generate) | Generate Alternatives (Generate) | Anticipate Changes (Generate) |
| Clarify Issues (Evaluate) | Test Causes (Evaluate) | Evaluate Alternatives (Evaluate) | Revise Plan (Evaluate) |
| Set Priority (Agree) | Gain Support (Agree) | Seek Agreement (Agree) | Gain Support (Agree) |

"Resolving even the most complex issue is fairly simple," Fox said. "You need to figure out what is happening: We call that situation assessment. Once you know what is happening, you need to figure out why it's happening: We call that problem solving. You need to come up with some potential solutions and decide which one is the best: That's decision making. And then you need to figure out how to implement the solution: That's the action planning stage. Within each of these stages, you need to gather information, generate ideas, evaluate the options, and seek agreement from the key stakeholders. The more creatures you have involved—the more proverbial squirrels, foxes, owls, and dogs—the better your ability to manage the issues you might face."

Deer waved a hoof. "You say that it's simple, but what we are facing is really complicated," she said.

"I agree that it's complicated. And while critical-thinking skills can make complex issues management simple, it does not make it easy," said Fox. "Using a framework such as this one will guard against falling into common thinking traps, will keep you on track, and will help justify your decisions to creatures who might not agree with you. Let me show you how it works."

# CHAPTER TEN

# SITUATION ASSESSMENT: WHAT IS HAPPENING?

Fox looked around the table. "Has anybody ever heard of a human called Yogi Berra?" Fox asked.

"That cartoon bear who loves picnics?" Dog asked.

"Close. That's Yogi Bear." Fox said, "Yogi Berra is a famous human baseball player. Berra was one of the greatest catchers of all times, but he is even better known for his quirky expressions. He said things like 'It ain't over till it's over,' and 'When you come to a fork in the road, take it.' One of my favorite Yogi-isms is: 'You can observe a lot by watching,'" Fox said.

Toad Jr. scoffed, "Well, that's kind of obvious, is it not?" he asked.

"It's not as obvious as creatures think," Fox said. "A lot of creatures—particularly intuitive-types like me—watch for a few minutes, jump to a conclusion, and then charge off to solve the problem."

"Sounds efficient to me," Badger said. As the guy in charge of printing the physical paper, he was always trying to think practically.

"Well, it is, unless you don't understand the situation well," Fox said. "I once did some work for a small not-for-profit organization that wanted to work in the developing world. They were concerned with the fact that animals were dying of malnutrition. What do you think the main problem was in the places where they were doing relief work?"

"Not enough food?" Deer asked.

"Seems obvious, doesn't it? Fox said. "Animals—humans are animals, too, you know—are hungry because there is not enough food. So what do you think a possible solution to not enough food might be?"

"Send food?" Hedgehog asked.

"Obvious, right?" Fox said. "One of their board members was the former CEO of a large grocery chain and he got his old competitors on board. They did a big food drive with all of the supermarkets and got transportation companies to donate their services to fly the food over to where creatures were hungry. And when they got there, how do you think the local leaders responded?"

"They were grateful?" Hedgehog asked.

"They were furious," Fox said.

"Huh?" Owl asked, echoing the others' confusion.

"You see," Fox continued, "the community was agriculture based. They needed help improving their farming and irrigation techniques. Sending food was a temporary measure and threatened to put the local farmers out of business, since they could not possibly compete with the free food."

"They got the situation wrong," Hedgehog said.

"Exactly. They got the situation wrong," Fox said. "The not-for-profit organization had a bias to look for a grocery solution because of the composition of their board. They were so eager to jump to action and do good that they did not spend enough time figuring out what was going on."

"They kind of acted like the wolf in that story you told me this morning," Hedgehog said.

"Precisely," Fox nodded and quickly recapped the fable of 'The Wolf and the Lamb' for Hedgehog's management team. "Just like the wolf, they asked the lamb a lot of questions. They did a feasibility study of food storage requirements, figured out how they'd distribute the food, and figured out the type of food that was most desired. But they asked only questions that supported their initial hunch."

"Did they ever consider anything other than a food solution?" Hedgehog asked.

"I reviewed the minutes of their board meetings. The treasurer, who was a forensic accountant for one of the major accounting firms, had asked if they ought to be considering any other solutions. He was a quiet fellow, however, and it looks like his opinion was overlooked. He was so frustrated that he ended up quitting the board."

"Oh dear," said Hedgehog. He looked over at Rabbit. She said that *The Bramblethorn Banner* had pursued her, but now Hedgehog was not so sure that she hadn't been keeping her eyes open for opportunities because of her frustration with how things were at *The Gazette*.

"So, how can you avoid falling into this trap?" Hedgehog asked.

"When we are thinking about something, the first thing we want to do is gather information about what is going on," answered Fox. "It's the first step in situation assessment, which is a fancy expression for what Yogi Berra called observing by watching. Before we jump to any conclusions about what the problem is, we want to identify all of the current issues. We want to know: What is happening? What is deviating from plan, goal, or budget? Animals with a preference for sensing are often really good at drilling down to discover the details about what is going on. In the case of our not-for-profit friends, they might have asked things like: Who is malnourished? How is malnourishment defined? How long has this been a problem? Where do they source their food now? How much food is available locally? What is the food supply chain in that area?"

Hedgehog nodded, "That makes sense."

"Let's work on figuring out what is going on with this paper as a group," Fox suggested. "You'll recall the critical thinking skills for issues management."

"The first thing you want to do is figure out what is going on," said Fox. "We call this skill situation assessment." He pointed to the card he distributed.

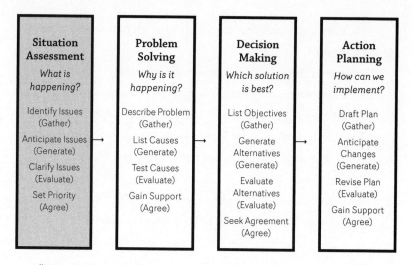

| Situation Assessment | Problem Solving | Decision Making | Action Planning |
|---|---|---|---|
| *What is happening?* | *Why is it happening?* | *Which solution is best?* | *How can we implement?* |
| Identify Issues (Gather) | Describe Problem (Gather) | List Objectives (Gather) | Draft Plan (Gather) |
| Anticipate Issues (Generate) | List Causes (Generate) | Generate Alternatives (Generate) | Anticipate Changes (Generate) |
| Clarify Issues (Evaluate) | Test Causes (Evaluate) | Evaluate Alternatives (Evaluate) | Revise Plan (Evaluate) |
| Set Priority (Agree) | Gain Support (Agree) | Seek Agreement (Agree) | Gain Support (Agree) |

"You need to identify any issues that affect you, your department, this newspaper, or this newspaper's customers. We can break it down into four steps: We identify or gather information about the current issues affecting the organization, we anticipate or generate some ideas about what issues might have an impact on the organization, we evaluate the issues to make sure we have identified the key ones, and we agree on what issues we want to address first. We use the critical thinking process—gather, generate, evaluate, agree—to make sure we have a good handle on whatever situation we face."

## Situation Assessment Process

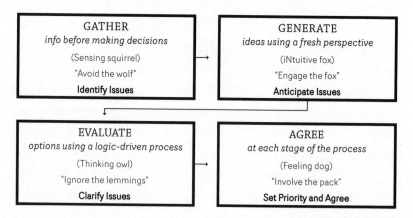

| GATHER | GENERATE |
|---|---|
| *info before making decisions* | *ideas using a fresh perspective* |
| (Sensing squirrel) | (iNtuitive fox) |
| "Avoid the wolf" | "Engage the fox" |
| **Identify Issues** | **Anticipate Issues** |

| EVALUATE | AGREE |
|---|---|
| *options using a logic-driven process* | *at each stage of the process* |
| (Thinking owl) | (Feeling dog) |
| "Ignore the lemmings" | "Involve the pack" |
| **Clarify Issues** | **Set Priority and Agree** |

"When Hedgehog hired me, I promised him more questions than answers. Here are some of the key questions to ask during the situation assessment stage," said Fox.

## Situation Assessment Key Questions

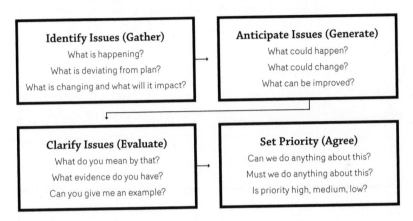

**Identify Issues (Gather)**
What is happening?
What is deviating from plan?
What is changing and what will it impact?

**Anticipate Issues (Generate)**
What could happen?
What could change?
What can be improved?

**Clarify Issues (Evaluate)**
What do you mean by that?
What evidence do you have?
Can you give me an example?

**Set Priority (Agree)**
Can we do anything about this?
Must we do anything about this?
Is priority high, medium, low?

"What I want to do for the next hour," Fox said, "is gather all of the issues the paper is facing. The time to evaluate those ideas will come later."

"Like brainstorming?" Dog asked.

"Precisely," said Fox. "Think about a buffet. We are going for quantity, not necessarily quality. The way I like to run a session like this is to go around the table two or three times and get everybody's input. I find that in traditional brainstorming sessions, the extraverted voices tend to dominate the introverted ones. I want to give everyone an equal chance to put his or her ideas forward."

"Are we looking at what is going on or what might go on?" asked Toad Jr. "I think that we have to look at things like shifting to more online content."

"That's a great point," said Fox. "Do any of know what made Wayne Gretzky such a great human hockey player?"

"Um, he was fast?" Toad Jr. asked. He liked to watch human sports.

"Yes! He was fast—both physically and mentally." Fox said. "By observing where the players were located and where the free spots were on the ice, he was able to figure out where the puck would most likely be. Lots of guys are fast enough to skate to where the puck is. Gretzky was able to skate to where the puck was going to be. In addition to gathering information about what is happening in the newspaper industry, we can also generate some ideas about what might be about to happen. We can blend the first and second steps here."

Fox isolated first and second steps of situation assessment and projected them on the overhead.

| Identify Issues (Gather) | Anticipate Issues (Generate) |
|---|---|
| What is happening? | What could happen? |
| What is deviating from plan? | What could change? |
| What is changing and what will it impact? | What can be improved? |

Fox continued, "Part of situation assessment is to gather information about what is happening. Who are our customers? How did our numbers compare to those last year? Who are our current competitors? What are other papers doing? We also need to anticipate issues that might be impacting us. What are readership numbers expected to do? Are there any trends or patterns in what creatures want to read? Are there other potential distribution channels? Given how things look now, where might things be heading?"

"My head hurts," Squirrel said.

Fox smiled. "I'm not surprised. As someone who has a preference for sensing, you will be more comfortable gathering facts about a situation—seeing where the puck is—than trying to figure out the issues you need to anticipate—seeing where the puck might be going. Both are valuable. If you don't know where the puck is, there is no way to assess where it's going to be."

"Isn't it silly to waste time on conjecture?" Badger asked.

"When we look for patterns and relationships, and make some educated guesses, it gives us some insight into the future. This is especially important in a rapidly evolving business such as yours. You might not know what will happen, but you will know about two or three things that are likely to occur. That way, you are less likely to be caught off guard," Fox said.

"Okay," Badger said tentatively.

Fox continued, "In the case of the not-for-profit organization I told you about, they might have explored how the political situation could impact the hunger situation, or the impact of climate, or the history of food production in the area and how that had changed. They might have looked at trends and asked if creatures fared better or worse in other locations or at other times. The nice thing about looking at both the sensory and intuitive side of a situation is that you don't miss out on anything. The intuitive types will allow you to see some possibilities and the sensers will ground those possibilities with hard facts."

Fox looked around the room. Badger, Hedgehog, Squirrel, and Fieldmouse did not look convinced.

"Something that might help the sensers in the room get more comfortable with looking into the future is a PESTEL analysis. Does anyone know what that is?"

"Something to do with cooking?" suggested Deer.

"Nope, not pestle, but P-E-S-T-E-L," Fox said. "It's an acronym standing for the trends that might impact your business," Fox said, jumping up out of his seat and scribbling on the white board.

> Political
>
> Economic
>
> Social
>
> Technological
>
> Environmental
>
> Legal/Regulatory

"That's helpful," said Fieldmouse. Squirrel nodded as well and was jotting down the acronym in his notebook.

"All right, let's get started. What is going on in the world of newspapers? What might be going on? Hedgehog, you're up first," Fox said.

Hedgehog thought for a moment.

"Our top clients are asking us for permanent ad rate discounts," he said.

"Perfect!" said Fox, typing on his laptop. "Got it. Let's go clockwise around the table. Squirrel, you're up."

"Competing advertising channels, particularly the Internet, are offering lower-cost advertising alternatives to our clients," said Squirrel.

"Yes!" said Fox, typing. "Deer?"

"We are losing newspaper subscribers," Deer said.

"Excellent!" Fox said. "Badger?"

"Newsprint costs have gone up and that makes the paper more expensive to produce."

"I'm loving this!" Fox proclaimed. "Owl?"

"If costs go up or revenue goes down, we will be breaking our bank covenants. They could pull our operating lines." Owl said grimly. A number of the animals around the table looked startled at this revelation.

"Okay," said Fox. "Coyote?"

"Our servers were down 2.4 percent of the time," Coyote explained. "That's bad."

"Extraordinary," said Fox, typing wildly. "Dog?"

"Sick days are up 4 percent. It's often an indicator of low morale," said Dog.

Hedgehog felt his heart lurch. He hated to think his employees were not happy.

"Toad Jr.," Fox said.

"We need to be doing more online. Our ad revenue is down. And it's going to stay that way. Recently, online ad revenue surpassed print news ad revenue. We need to tap into that revenue stream," Toad Jr. said.

"Alrighty," Fox said, typing. "Rabbit?"

"The sections that seem to attract the most readers are local news and personal finance tips. Suzy Sparrow, the queen of personal finance, is willing to write for us, but she won't do it for free. I also need some junior reporters to cover the neighborhood beat. We have to compete with those hyper-local papers that send photographers to cover store openings and high school sporting events. Everyone seems to love that."

"Got it!" Fox said. "Fieldmouse?"

Fieldmouse looked surprised to be asked, "Um, but I'm just the assistant," he said.

"Nonsense, you understand string theory and have probably read more business books than I have," said Hedgehog firmly. "What is one issue you see the paper facing."

Fieldmouse thought for a minute. "Everyone is printing our content. Most things are off the newswire, which everyone has access to. Or if we do have a good story, you see it replicated online."

The animals around the table remained quiet. Rabbit folded her paws across her chest.

Fox was typing. "That's terrific," he said finally. "Really terrific."

"All right," Fox said. "Let's go around the table again, gathering one more issue from each of you."

Fox sat back down in his chair in front of his laptop, ready to type. "All right," he said. "Hedgehog, what else is going on?"

The animals offered their thoughts and opinions in turn. Then there was a more open brainstorming session where animals volunteered ideas. The most vocal contributors were Toad Jr., Dog, Rabbit, Squirrel, Deer, and—somewhat surprisingly, given his initial reluctance—Fieldmouse. Fox guessed that all of these animals were extraverts. Everyone made a point or two, however, and Fox had to type as quickly as he could. He found himself wishing that he had more digits.

"Alrighty," he said. "Does everyone feel like they have had an opportunity to share all of their points?"

The animals nodded.

Fox plugged his laptop into the boardroom projector and showed the management team the issues they'd raised.

"I have recorded your ideas on a situation assessment worksheet. When you are making a big decision, not only does having a process to capture your data help keep you organized, but it acts as a paper trail to help bring those not in the room on board," Fox said.

Reading the list made Hedgehog want to dig a hole and crawl into it. It seemed like things were dire.

"Fox, can I see you in the hall for a minute?" he asked.

"Absolutely. Five-minute break, everyone," Fox announced. "Take a bio break or take a few minuts to review what I've captured on the following situation assessment worksheet."

| Identify (Gather) Anticipate(Generate) | Clarify (Evaluate) | Set Priority (Agree) | | |
|---|---|---|---|---|
| | | Can we fix? | Must we fix? | Priority |
| Top ad clients asking for permanent discounts | | | | |
| Competitors (Internet) offering lower cost ad alternative to our customers | | | | |
| Losing newspaper subscribers | | | | |
| Newsprint costs up | | | | |
| If above happens, will break bank covenants | | | | |
| Online servers down 2.4 percent of time | | | | |
| Sick days up (poor morale?) | | | | |
| Ad revenue down | | | | |
| Online ad revenue surpassed newspaper ad revenue | | | | |
| Need increased budget for hyper-local and personal finance writers | | | | |
| Paper lacks compelling/ inspiring content | | | | |
| Too much of current content can be found elsewhere | | | | |
| Ad customers appear to be colluding to request block price decreases | | | | |
| 38 percent of readers have visited the newspaper's website | | | | |
| Lost classified ads to EggsList. | | | | |
| 40 percent of readers trust the newspaper. | | | | |
| Paper irrelevant | | | | |
| The chickens who work in the press area keep threatening to unionize | | | | |
| Specialized media seems to be a trend | | | | |
| If interest rates increase, our costs will go up | | | | |
| Gazette lacks identity | | | | |
| New health and safety regulations mean all workers need additional training | | | | |
| 6 other regional newspapers have gone bankrupt this year | | | | |
| TJ's celebrity gossip Web page is most widely read on site | | | | |
| Flashbulb's free hyper-local newspaper is eyeing Toad Hollow as part of its expansion plan | | | | |
| Forest fires expected to cause increase in price of newsprint | | | | |
| Bankers would welcome "digital media play" | | | | |
| Online ad rates cheaper | | | | |
| The government grant program that subsidized summer interns has been cancelled | | | | |
| The local news and sports sections are read most often but creatures asking for more "lifestyle" articles | | | | |
| Production targeted for cost-cutting | | | | |

# CHAPTER ELEVEN

# SITUATION ASSESSMENT: CLARIFYING THE PROBLEM

"What's up?" he asked Hedgehog when they were in the hallway with the door closed behind them.

"Is this is good idea?" Hedgehog asked.

"What do you mean?" asked Fox.

"This," Hedgehog waved one of his paws. "Is this whole thing a good idea? I mean, it makes me look kind of stupid to have my staff point out everything that is wrong with the paper, doesn't it?"

Fox shook his head. "It makes them feel like you value their opinion. Believe me, your staff is very aware of what is wrong with the paper. And they don't blame you for it. Did you start that forest fire that threatens to drive up paper prices?"

"Of course not," Hedgehog said.

"In business, the smart creatures are often worried that the guys driving the bus have no idea what is going on. They will feel relieved to know that you want to know everything that is of concern. It shows you trust them and you are all on the same team," Fox said.

"It feels scary," said Hedgehog.

"That's why most creatures dislike change so much," said Fox. "It's uncomfortable to try doing things a new way."

Hedgehog sighed. "I guess we had better go back inside," he said.

\*\*\*

"All right, so we captured a bunch of the issues that are affecting, or could be affecting, this newspaper," said Fox. "What do we need to do next?"

Owl raised her wing, "Well, a lot of these things seem really vague. I'd like a lot more facts and details to know how valid—and how serious—these various issues are."

"Alrighty," Fox said. "So at this point you have *gathered* some facts about what is going on and you have *generated* some ideas about what might be going on. Now you need to *evaluate* the information by clarifying the data. So, does anyone know how to get started?"

"I think that we need to challenge some of the information on the worksheet," said Rabbit.

"What kinds of questions would you ask to challenge some of the data?" Fox asked.

"Well, I'd ask things like 'What evidence do you have?' and 'What do we mean?'" Rabbit said.

"That would help clarify things. It's also valuable to ask 'What do you mean by that?' or 'Can you give me an example?' This evaluative thinking can prevent us from acting on potentially wrong assumptions," confirmed Fox.

He isolated the evaluate step of situation assessment and projected it on the screen:

---

**Clarify Issues (Evaluate)**
What do you mean by that?
What evidence do you have?
Can you give me an example?

---

"What personality types are likely to feel most comfortable with this process?" Fox asked.

"Thinkers," Owl said quickly. "I love this stuff."

"Okay, so I'm going to ask each of you to provide some evidence for your earlier statements. This is the chance for everyone to question the issues and make sure they are grounded by facts." Fox explained. "Hedgehog. You're up first again. You said that the top ad clients asked for permanent discounts. What do you mean by that?"

"Well," said Hedgehog, "it's my understanding from Squirrel that Raccoon of Raccoon Auto Mart, Bear of Big Bear Real Estate, Turtle of Turtle Travel, and Magpie of Magpie Jewelers all demanded a 15 percent ad discount or they'll pull their business from us."

"How much business do they do with us?" Toad Jr. asked.

"Squirrel, this is more your area of expertise," Hedgehog said. "Do you mind answering?"

Squirrel flipped through his notebook, where he took notes whenever he spoke to clients. He was a very detail-oriented fellow. "When they asked for the discount, I pulled together a few numbers," he said. "Here it is: Raccoon does 7 percent of our retail ad revenues, Big Bear does just over 6 percent. Turtle used to be our biggest advertiser, but since the recession he books just under 5 percent. Magpie does just over 3 percent. Collectively, they do about 1.5 million dollars in ad revenue a year. A 15 percent discount reduces our revenues by $225,000."

"So if we offer them a 15 percent discount on a continuing basis, what does that do to our covenants?" Rabbit asked.

"We might break them," Owl said. "A $225,000 hit to the top line with no adjustment to costs could decrease our operating margins below the bank's threshold if any other negatives occurred."

"So we can't extend the discounts," Coyote said.

"During this stage we don't have to draw any conclusions," Fox reminded them. "Remember, we are simply assessing the situation."

Fox typed the clarifying points into his laptop and projected the amended table using the projector:

| Identify (Gather) Anticipate(Generate) | Clarify (Evaluate) | Set Priority (Agree) | | |
|---|---|---|---|---|
| | | Can we fix? | Must we fix? | Priority |
| Top ad clients asking for permanent discounts | Raccoon, Bear, Turtle, Magpie (top 20 percent of ad revenue) want 15 percent discount ($225,000) | | | |

"Does everybody see how grounding things with facts makes the issues a lot more clear? Okay, let's go back to Squirrel. Squirrel, you said that competitors are offering lower cost alternatives to your customers. How do you know this?" Fox asked.

"Well," Squirrel said, "when I was talking to Turtle of Turtle Travel, he told me that he can advertise online for a fraction of the cost. I did some more research into this and discovered that our standard newspaper ad costs 20 times more than an online ad seen by the same number of readers."

"But do those ads work?" Rabbit demanded. "I just ignore them."

"Well, online ads are seen by a lot of readers," Squirrel answered. "But the value of those readers might not be the same because they are so overexposed to ads. I read a report that a print reader is worth 228 times more than an online reader. But that was revenue per reader. In other words, that's the value of the reader to us. Finding out how much that reader is worth to our advertisers is different. I haven't been able to find the data yet."

"Sounds like it means that our ads are not priced too high," Owl said. "Presumably there is some relationship between revenue and perceived value."

"Well," said Squirrel, "there is probably some truth to that. If the advertisers thought we brought no value to the table, they'd simply stop placing ads. The thing is, we need to understand who is reading us and why, and how that impacts their buying decisions. We can then use that information to sell our ads to customers."

"Got it," Fox said as he finished typing. "Deer, you said we are losing newspaper subscribers. Quantify that, please."

"Well," Deer said, "we are losing subscribers at a rate of about 3 percent per year. We've lost a huge number of sales from newspaper boxes and convenience stores. Now that everyone has tablets and smart phones, nobody buys a paper to read on the train anymore."

"Is a 3 percent decline normal for the industry?" Coyote asked.

"Well, we lost a lot of subscribers after Glenwide went bankrupt in the mortgage-backed securities crash. A lot of Toad Hollow creatures lost their jobs and the daily newspaper delivery was seen as a luxury. Our numbers went down 10 percent per year the two years following the crash. We've stabilized. A 3 percent decline is about average for regional papers like ours. Some papers are losing more. Some specialty papers, especially the free ones, are growing in readership."

"Thanks, Deer," said Fox.

"No worries, darling," she responded.

Fox chuckled. "We've got a live one here," he said.

"Badger," Fox said, "newsprint costs are up. How much?" he asked.

"3 percent," Badger said.

"Can't we hedge against that?" asked Toad Jr.

"Owl?" Badger asked.

Owl shook her head. "Because forest fires have been decreasing the supply, the entire industry was hit with a 3 percent increase this year," she said. "Forwards, futures, we've tried it all. You can monkey around a bit with smoothing your cash flow, but when prices are up, they're up."

Owl shook her head. "We'll break our bank covenants."

"Owl, what's up with the bank covenants? It seems they are always in peril," Fox said.

"Basically, if there is a $250,000 decrease in revenue or increase in costs, we break our covenants," Owl said. "A $225,000 hit to ad revenues doesn't leave a lot of margin for error. The bank will not adjust things unless we change our business model. They've lost faith in print media."

"Okay, Coyote," Fox said, wanting to move the conversation forward. "Let's talk servers."

"Right," said Coyote. "Ever since Toad Jr. set up his celebrity blog, we've been having trouble keeping our servers working well. We have experienced 2.4 percent downtime, most of which happens when Toad uploads new photos of Maggie Muskrat."

After appearing in the Woodland award-winning film, *The Hunted,* the young starlet had been an active Internet search. Toad Jr. and Maggie were pals from his photography days, and they still got together whenever they were both in the same city. She needed constant publicity and he needed celebrity content, so the relationship worked well for both of them.

"If we plan to move more of our business online, we need to move to cloud computing," Coyote explained.

"What's that going to cost?" Badger asked. Badger was always being asked to trim the cost of physically producing the paper and always wanted to know how the newspaper was otherwise spending its money.

"There is no capital expenditure to move to the cloud, but we really need some new hardware and updated software. Ours is held together with duct tape and wishes," Coyote said. "Plus, I will need another animal in my department if we are moving more things online. I have to cover his or her salary. That's at least $75,000."

"We need to hire editorial staff!" Rabbit objected. "What's the point of finding a way to put content online if there is no content in the first place!"

Toad Jr. stood up in his chair getting ready to shout. Fox interjected.

"Again, we are simply clarifying the issues right now. We will all have a chance to make some decisions later," Fox assured the group. "Okay, Dog. What's up with morale?"

"Well," said Dog, "sick days are up 4 percent this year, which is quite a jump. An increase in sick days is often correlated with poor morale. Animals don't feel like coming into work, so they call in sick. Since the layoffs a couple of years ago, everyone has been working twice as hard. The employees are burned out."

"Anyone have any comments?" Fox asked.

"The chickens are sick all the time," said Badger. "It makes getting the paper out on time really difficult."

"Well, I don't think morale is great," said Toad Jr, "but there was an awful flu virus going around this past year. I think creatures were authentically sick. I never get sick and even I was out for a couple of days last winter."

"Could that be possible?" Fox asked Dog.

"A 4 percent increase in sick days is a big jump," Dog said, "but it's possible a serious flu could account for that. Still, I think it's worth noting that employees are feeling overworked."

"Perfect," said Fox. "Okay, Squirrel, we need more information on ad revenue."

"Well," said Squirrel, leaning back in his chair and putting his feet up on the table. "Ad revenue is down 5 percent from last year. That puts us at the high end of regional newspaper averages, which ran a decline of 3 to 5 percent."

"All right," said Fox, typing. "And how does that compare to online revenue?"

"Well, we have no online ad revenue, but generally online ad revenue is growing like gangbusters. I read in the latest *Toadstool Research* media report that online ad revenue surpassed newspaper ad revenue for the first time last year."

"I read that too," Rabbit said. "And while that's true for the big national newspapers, it's not true of the local or regional ones like *The Toad Hollow Gazette*."

"True," said Toad Jr. "But given our ad rate decline and online's increasing share of the ad market, I expect local online will surpass local newspapers next year."

"That's conjecture!" said Rabbit.

"I'll note it as such," said Fox. "Okay, Rabbit. What's up with editorial?"

"Toad's beloved Toadstool Research report noted that two key areas of growth for newspapers are hyper-local features—think regional bake-sales, fires, high school sports scores, break-in reports—and personal finance. I can hire Suzy Sparrow to do an exclusive weekly column for us. Her column will focus on personal finance for animals going through tough economic times like the creatures of Toad Hollow. This is the kind of thing I think might play well online too. She is wildly popular and her books are best-sellers."

"What does she want to get paid?" Toad Jr. asked.

"She's asking for $75,000 per year for an exclusive weekly column," said Rabbit.

"That's crazy!" Badger protested. "I could hire two more chickens to run the presses for that much. Then morale might not be so poor in my area!"

"Unless Suzy Sparrow immediately generates more readers and attracts more advertisers, hiring her will cause us to break our covenants," Owl reminded the group.

"And you think you need a junior reporter in addition to Ms. Sparrow?" Fox asked.

"Yes." Rabbit nodded. "If we want hyper-local coverage, we need to be able to send out a junior reporter when the proverbial cat gets stuck in the proverbial tree. I can get somebody right out of school for $35,000."

"That's another chicken able to work the presses!" Badger exclaimed.

"No offense, Badger," Rabbit said, "but chickens don't sell newspapers."

"Let's not make things personal," Fox said. "Remember, we will be discussing these issues in greater depth later on, okay? Fieldmouse, the paper is not inspiring you. Explain."

"Okay," Fieldmouse said, "we offer the same content I can find anywhere. Most news that we print is stuff off the newswire. The sports pages tell me the same information—scores and highlights—that I saw the night before on television. At tax time, I'll get the same information I get from my tax guy. Every Mother's Day, I know I'm going to see recipes for breakfast in bed. There is very little unique content. If I'm going to invest the time to read an article, then I want it to really say something. I like reading *The Bee-Conomist* because I always come away with in-depth knowledge and a fresh perspective. That has value for me."

"Wow!" said Fox, typing madly.

Fox went around the table again until each issue that had been raised during the issue-gathering and generation stage had been further clarified. He then projected the results up onto the screen.

| Identify (Gather) Anticipate(Generate) | Clarify (Evaluate) | Set Priority (Agree) | | |
|---|---|---|---|---|
| | | Can we fix? | Must we fix? | Priority |
| Top ad clients asking for permanent discounts | Raccoon, Bear, Turtle, Magpie (top 20 percent of ad revenue) want 15 percent discount ($225,000) | | | |
| Competitors (internet) offering lower cost ad alternative to our customers | Newspaper ads 20X cost. (228X value?) | | | |
| Losing newspaper subscribers | 3 percent per year | | | |
| Newsprint costs up | 3 percent per year | | | |
| If above happens, will break bank covenant | If revenues down $250,000 or costs up $250,000 with no offset | | | |
| Online servers down 2.4 percent of time | 2.4 percent vs industry 0.3 percent, cloud and extra IT person = $75,000 | | | |
| Sick days up (poor morale?) | Sick days up 4 percent, was particularly tough flu season, morale seems low | | | |
| Ad revenue down | *Gazette* down 5 percent vs. 3-5 percent per year industry | | | |
| Online ad revenue surpassed newspaper ad revenue | National online ad revenue > national newpaper revenue | | | |
| Need increased budget for hyperlocal and personal finance writers | Suzy Sparrow + jr. writer = $110,000 | | | |

*Continued on page 114*

| | | | | |
|---|---|---|---|---|
| Paper lacks compelling/ inspiring content | anecdotal | | | |
| Too much content can be found elsewhere | anecdotal | | | |
| Ad customers appear to be colluding to request block price decreases | 4 golf buddies asked for discounts | | | |
| Only 38 percent of readers have visited the newspaper's website | Too little content | | | |
| Lose classified ads to EggsList | lose 10 percent classified ad revenue/year | | | |
| 40 percent of readers trust the newspaper | 10 percent trust blogs— Toadstool Research | | | |
| Paper irrelevant | Only 30 percent of Toad Hollow residents read paper daily | | | |
| The chickens who work in the press area keep threatening to unionize | Have told Badger but not Dog in AR | | | |
| Specialized media seems to be a trend | New papers focusing on hyper-local, sports, and personal finance | | | |
| If interest rates increase, our costs will go up | If rates go up half a percent we fall below covenant | | | |
| *Gazette* lacks identity | What are we? What is our role in Toad Hollow? In world? | | | |
| New health and safety regulations mean all workers need additional training | 2 hours per employee ($20,000) | | | |
| 6 regional newspapers have gone bankrupt this year | Located in towns affected by recession | | | |
| TJ's celebrity gossip Web page is most widely read on site | 250,000 daily readers vs. 400 daily readers | | | |
| *Flashbulb* free hyper-local paper eyeing Toad Hollow as part of expansion plans | Anecdotal | | | |
| Bankers would welcome "digital media play" | Anecdotal | | | |
| The government grant program that allowed them to subsidize summer interns has been cancelled | Immediately | | | |
| The local news and sports sections are read most but creatures asking for more "lifestyle" articles | Anecdotal | | | |
| Need to cost cut in production | Production costs are only 39 percent of total costs, consider SG&A | | | |

"Okay," said Fox. "As you can see from the board, we have a lot of issues on the table. Since we can't take on everything at once, we have to rank the issues and tackle them in the order of importance. We've been able to gather, generate, and even evaluate the information somewhat independently of one another," said Fox. "But at this stage we need to reach consensus so that we can start to deal with the most pressing issues."

"Who should be involved in making the decision? Is there a vote? Is it majority wins or do you need unanimity? Is there a veto?" Rabbit asked.

"Well, that's up to you," Fox said. "Remember, the whole point of involving the pack is to gain buy-in and to move things forward."

"If we need to reach consensus on everything, we might as well hang up the bankruptcy sign on the door now. Consensus is impossible," Deer protested.

Fox smiled. "Well, you might not be able to achieve 100 percent consensus, but for creatures with a preference for feeling, it's important to consider everyone involved. As I told Hedgehog earlier, there are two things that are needed for a project to succeed: getting the right solution and having the commitment to implement it. Engagement is hugely important and it rarely comes from vetoing something others deem important."

A number of the animals around the table nodded their heads.

"Okay, so when it comes to setting priority, we need to focus on a few key questions," said Fox.

---

**Set Priority (Agree)**

Can we do anything about this?

Must we do anything about this?

Is priority high, medium, low?

---

Fox continued: "It's important to establish if we can do anything about a situation. If it's beyond our control, all we can do is put measures in place to minimize the risk. Our first issue is that the top 20 percent of ad clients—Raccoon, Bear, Turtle and Magpie—want a 15 percent reduction in ad rates. That reduces revenue by $225,000 and bumps against our bank covenants. Can you do anything about this?"

Squirrel waved his paws in the air. Fox pointed to him. "We can't prevent them from asking for the discount, but we can either lower rates 15 percent, which costs us $225,000 or risk losing 20 percent of our ad business, which costs us $1,500,000."

"Everyone agree?" Fox asked.

Most of the animals nodded their heads.

"Do you have to do anything about this? Or can you just ignore it for now?" Fox asked.

"We have to act now," Squirrel said. "Now that they are all in cahoots, they have to save face by getting what they want. We have to give them something or risk losing 100 percent of their business," he said.

"How do we know they are not bluffing?" Toad Jr. said. "I was raised to believe that if you don't ask, you don't get. As a result, I ask for the moon all the time, but I don't necessarily expect to get it," he said.

Hedgehog made a mental note to remember that during salary reviews.

Toad Jr. continued. "If everybody is saying, 'Newspapers are dying, newspapers are dying' maybe it makes sense for us to take a stand and say, 'They are not dying, and our rates stand as they are.' We should take a position of strength."

"Wait a minute," interrupted Rabbit. "You are the one telling us that newspapers are dying and losing money and we need to move online right away," she said.

"That's true," Toad Jr. said. "I do believe that, but I don't think we need to signal to our customers that it's over."

"So, we should just tell them that we don't want to play ball?" Squirrel asked.

Hedgehog thought for a moment. "What if we added some value to their current offering. Like they get free Internet advertising on Toad Jr.'s blog?"

"I love it!" said Toad Jr. "It will get them to sample the power of digital media but keep them as print clients."

"I love it because we won't break covenants," said Owl.

Coyote waved his paw in the air. "I need to move to the cloud, though. And I'll need some extra help with IT."

"But $75,000 for an upgrade we need anyway, is cheaper than a $225,000 discount or $1,500,000 revenue loss if we lose the advertisers," said Owl.

Fox interrupted. "I love the way you are thinking. You are leaping into problem-solving mode, which is fantastic. I know that you are going to have solutions that are amazing. However, I want to finish up with the situation assessment and discover our most pressing issue. Then we can go into problem-solving mode. Promise!" he grinned.

Fox pointed to the situation assessment matrix on the overhead screen. "I will write a *Y* in the first column to indicate that, yes, we *can* do something about the issue and a *Y* in the second column to show that, yes, we *must* do something about the issue. For the third column, we need to determine priority. Is dealing with the ad discount issue high, medium or low priority?" Fox asked.

"High!" said Squirrel. "Whether we extend the discounts or not, 20 percent of our advertising is tied up in making some sort of decision."

"Does anybody disagree?" Fox asked.

Nobody disagreed.

"Who are the key creatures who need to be involved in solving this issue?" Fox asked.

"Hmm," said Squirrel. "I'd say me, Hedgehog, Owl—to run the numbers—and maybe Toad Jr. if we are going to do something online."

He wrote *H* on the situation assessment matrix to indicate that the issue was a high-priority one and then wrote the name of the animals involved:

| Identify (Gather) Anticipate(Generate) | Clarify (Evaluate) | Set Priority (Agree) | | |
|---|---|---|---|---|
| | | Can we fix? | Must we fix? | Priority |
| Top ad clients asking for permanent discounts | Raccoon, Bear, Turtle, Magpie (top 20 percent of ad revenue) want 15 percent discount ($225,000) | Y | Y | H Hhog Squrl Owl Toad |

"Okay," said Fox. "Let's run through these other issues the same way. Squirrel, you raised the issue that competitors—primarily online—are offering significantly lower-cost advertising alternatives to your customers. Can you do anything about that?"

"We can respond to that by lowering our prices," said Squirrel.

"True, but I did not ask that. I asked if you *can* do anything about low Internet advertising costs?" Fox said, smiling encouragingly.

"No, we really can't. We can show our clients that we offer better value, but we can't do anything about the cost of online ads," agreed Squirrel.

"All right. So this is an issue of which we need to be aware since it is driving our customers to ask for discounts. But since there is nothing we can do about online advertising costs, we don't need to waste time trying to change them," Fox said.

"It's like that saying!" exclaimed Fieldmouse. "My uncle has it on a fridge magnet, 'Grant me the serenity to accept the things I cannot change, the courage to change the things I can, and the wisdom to know the difference.'"

"Precisely!" said Fox. "Once we determine that we can't do anything about an issue, we can move on."

Fox continued, "Next, we are losing newspaper subscribers at a rate of 3 percent per year. Deer, I think that you raised this issue. Can we do anything about this?"

"Yes," said Deer. "When we offer a promotion of some sort, the subscription numbers go up."

"I disagree!" said Toad Jr. "Over time, all newspapers are losing subscribers. Young creatures don't read papers. There will come a point in time when you won't even be able to give it away."

"But what about the growth of specialty papers?" asked Rabbit.

"If we don't believe that we can do anything about increasing subscribers in the short term at the very least, then I think we should just all go home," said Hedgehog. "I still believe in newspapers. The economy of Toad Hollow is coming back. We will benefit from that improvement."

"Hear, hear!" exclaimed Rabbit.

"Alrighty, I think it's worth keeping on the table then," Fox said. "So, if we can do something about it, must we do something about it?"

"Yes!" Hedgehog said. "We must stop the bleeding and start increasing our readership."

Toad Jr. shook his head. "I think it's a lost cause, but who am I to stand in the way," he said.

"What is the priority?" Fox asked.

"High!" Hedgehog insisted.

"Higher or lower than dealing with the request for ad rate adjustments."

Hedgehog thought a moment. "Well, given that ad revenues are 53 percent of our revenues and circulation is 45 percent, and given that our advertisers seem more focused on asking for a discount because of cheap online alternatives than asking for a discount because our readership is declining, I'd have to say it's medium priority in comparison. They are using it as an excuse to renegotiate our contract, but I think it's just an excuse."

"Anybody disagree?" asked Fox.

"I can live with that," said Deer. "As long as I don't get ambushed at performance review time."

"That's one of the benefits of doing an exercise like this," said Fox. "When it's clear to everyone what we are working on as an organization, there are fewer surprises. You've heard it from the CEO that fixing the ad rate issue is more of a priority than stopping the loss of subscribers. As the circulation manager, it might be smart for you to get on some cross-functional teams so that you can make a contribution to some higher-priority areas."

"Good advice," said Deer.

"Okay, so who is in charge of improving circulation?" asked Fox.

"Um," Deer said, pausing to think, "I am, and Hedgehog and Rabbit. We need Rabbit to produce pieces that creatures want to read. Maybe do some new features or something?"

"Hedgehog? Rabbit? Are you on board with that?" Fox asked. "Anybody else think they should be involved?"

"As the promotions guy, I think that I should be very involved," Toad Jr. said.

"I agree," said Deer. "I want to find out more about how we can use the marketing budget to reach potential subscribers."

"Great!" said Fox, typing furiously.

"Okay, Badger, I think that the issue you raised was that newsprint costs are up," Fox said. "Can you do anything about this?"

Badger shook his head. "Owl and I have talked about doing things like buying options or hedging our position by investing to minimize our risk. I think we've done a lot to smooth the costs and make the risk more manageable, but in the end it's not something we have much control over unless we want to shrink the size of the paper."

"So are you okay shelving the issue for now?" Fox asked.

"Yes," Badger said. "If we don't figure out this ad thing and 20 percent of that business walks out the door, the price of newsprint won't really matter, will it."

Fox went around the room and the group had to reach agreement on all of the issues raised. When they were finished, he bolded all of the high-priority items and projected the situation assessment chart up on the overhead:

| Identify (Gather) Anticipate(Generate) | Clarify (Evaluate) | Set Priority (Agree) | | |
|---|---|---|---|---|
| | | Can we fix? | Must we fix? | Priority |
| **Top ad clients asking for permanent discounts** | **Raccoon, Bear, Turtle, Magpie (top 20 percent of ad revenue) want 15 percent discount ($225,000)** | Y | Y | **H** Hhog Squrl Owl TJ |
| Competitors (Internet) offering lower-cost ad alternative to our customers | Newspaper ads 20X cost. (228X value?) | N | | |
| Losing newspaper subscribers | 3 percent per year | Y | Y | M Deer Rabbit TJ |
| Newsprint costs up | 3 percent per year | N | | |
| **If above happens, will break bank covenant** | **If revenues down or costs up with no offset** | Y | Y | **H** Owl Hhog Board |
| Online servers down 2.4 percent of time | 2.4 percent vs. industry 0.3 percent, cloud and extra IT person | Y | Y | M Coyote Owl |
| Sick days up (poor morale?) | Sick days up 4 percent, was particularly tough flu season, morale seems low | Y | N | |
| Ad revenue down | *Gazette* down 5 percent vs. 3-5 percent per year for industry | Y | Y | M Squrl Owl Rabbit TJ |
| Online ad revenue surpassed newspaper ad revenue | National online ad revenue > national newspaper revenue | N | | |
| Need increased budget for hyperlocal and personal finance writers | Suzy Sparrow + jr. writer | Y | Y | M Rabbit Hhog |
| Paper lacks compelling/ inspiring content | anecdotal | Y | N | |
| Too much content can be found elsewhere | anecdotal | Y | N | |
| Ad customers appear to be colluding to request block price decreases | 4 golf buddies asked for discounts | N | | |
| Only 38 percent of readers have visited the newspaper's website | Too little content | Y | Y | L TJ Rabbit Coyote |
| Lose classified ads to EggsList. | Lose 10 percent classified ad revenue/year | N | | |
| 40 percent of readers trust the newspaper. | 10 percent trust blogs— Toadstool Research | N | | |
| **Paper irrelevant** | **Only 30 percent of Toad Hollow residents read paper daily** | Y | Y | **H** Rabbit Deer |

*Continued on page 122*

| | | | | |
|---|---|---|---|---|
| The chickens who work in the press area keep threatening to unionize | Have told Badger but not Dog in AR | Y | Y | M Dog Hhog Badger |
| Specialized media seems to be a trend | New papers focusing on hyperlocal, sports, and personal finance | N | | |
| If interest rates increase, our costs will go up | If rates go up half a percent we fall below covenant | N | | |
| *Gazette* lacks identity. | **What are we? What is our role in Toad Hollow? In world?** | **Y** | **Y** | **H Hhog Board** |
| New health and safety regulations mean all workers need additional training | 2 hours per employee | Y | Y | M Dog |
| 6 other regional newspapers have gone bankrupt this year. | Located in towns affected by recession | N | | |
| TJ's celebrity gossip Web page is most widely read on site | 40,000 daily readers | Y | N | |
| *Flashbulb* free hyperlocal paper eyeing Toad Hollow as part of expansion plans | Anecdotal | N | | |
| Bankers would welcome "digital media play" | Anecdotal | N | | |
| The government grant program that allowed them to subsidize summer interns has been cancelled | Immediately | N | | |
| The local news and sports sections are read most but creatures asking for more "lifestyle" articles | Anecdotal | Y | Y | L Rabbit |
| Production targeted for cost-cutting | Production costs are only 39 percent of total costs, consider SG&A | Y | N | |

"Okay," said Fox. "So we've raised a lot of important issues, but we can't do anything about some of them. While it's good to keep the information in mind—these issues may impact areas where we do have some control—there is no point spending a lot of time worrying about them. Take the threat of higher interest rates, as an example. You have no impact on what the rates are. The issue simply highlights a need to remain within the bank covenants—something that will be much harder to do if rates pop up. Does that make sense?"

The managers around the table nodded.

Fox continued. "Some of the issues are ones within your control but they are not something that you *have* to do something about.

It's good to have these on your radar screen so that you know that they are a potential problem before they become a full-blown disaster. It can also show an opportunity. It's good to know, for example, that Toad's Web page attracts the same number of readers that the print paper has. Perhaps this represents an opportunity to grow our readership. Perhaps some of those celebrity-column readers can read other parts of the paper online. But it's not something we have to deal with today."

Toad Jr. nodded his head.

Fox continued. "Then, there are a number of issues that are important, but take lower priority than some of the other issues. I've made a note of who is responsible for these issues. Dealing with these issues might become part of long-range planning. It's better to be able to deal with these issues before they become problems. Finally, there are the important, high-priority issues we must deal with immediately. I'll just press this button here on my laptop and I will make the other issues disappear like magic."

"Voilà! This is why creatures like consultants and coaches so much," he grinned. "We can make your problems simply disappear."

| Identify (Gather) Anticipate(Generate) | Clarify (Evaluate) | Set Priority (Agree) | | |
|---|---|---|---|---|
| | | Can we fix? | Must we fix? | Priority |
| Top ad clients asking for permanent discounts | Raccoon, Bear, Turtl e, Magpie (top 20 percent of ad revenue) want 15 percent discount ($225,000) | Y | Y | H Hhog Squrl Owl TJ |
| If above happens, will break bank covenant | If revenues down or costs up with no offset | Y | Y | H Owl Hhog Board |
| Paper irrelevant | Only 30 percent of Toad Hollow residents read paper daily | Y | Y | H Rabbit Deer |
| *Gazette* lacks identity | What are we? What is our role in Toad Hollow? In world? | Y | Y | H Hhog Board |

Fieldmouse shot his paw up in the air. "How do we know we have the right issues on the board?" he asked.

"Excellent question, my friend," Fox said. "The truth is, there is no 'right' answer for everyone. Another newspaper could be doing this exact analysis right now and come up with a completely different set of problems, even if they have most of the same issues. The key part of critical thinking is that we go through a process to make sure that we avoid the typical traps. We avoid the wolf by making sure we gather up all the relevant information and don't simply jump to conclusions. We engage the fox by generating some ideas using a fresh perspective. Often this is accomplished by inviting creatures we might not normally include in the process. We ignore the lemmings by evaluating the information before we act. We might have assumed that our big problem is that the Internet charges 1/20th of what newsprint does for ads. When we probe further and see that we offer up to 228 times the value, suddenly we feel less inclined to slash our prices to compete, no? And then, finally, we involve the pack. We need to find the most significant issues and increase our commitment to resolve them. This thinking process makes sure that we've thought critically about the issues and that they are generally sound. The process also makes sure that those with differing views have a chance to have their thoughts aired. Remember, we will never reach 100 percent consensus, but it's a bit like democratically run elections. If everyone feels that the process is fair, even if we are not thrilled with the outcome, we can accept it. Some animals may feel so strongly that their views were not accepted that they leave for another organization with a better cultural fit. And that's okay too, over the long haul."

"So just the process of doing this will make everybody feel more involved?" asked Dog.

"Why don't you tell me?" asked Fox.

"I was not aware that things were so tight financially," said Badger. "Before coming into this meeting, I thought unionizing chickens was our biggest problem. This has been helpful."

"And I wanted to get new resources because the last IT manager got fired when our system crashed. Even though I am relatively new here, it makes sense that we focus on content, before we focus on distributing that content," said Coyote.

"Well, I think it's great that we have a publisher who lets us have input," said Dog. "I worked for *The Bramblethorn Banner* before I came here, and they did not let anyone have a say in anything."

"I didn't know you worked for *The Banner*," said Rabbit, sitting up in her seat. That was the paper that had made her the offer to join as editor in chief.

"Yup, for a few years," Dog said. "They promised me the moon and told me that AR was a central function there and I'd be on the senior management team. In the end, all they wanted me to do was fire creatures and order the donuts on teambuilding day."

Rabbit was concerned. The main reason she was entertaining the offer was that they were offering her far more autonomy than she had at *The Gazette*. Dog's comments were troubling.

Hedgehog, knowing that Rabbit was still contemplating *The Banner*'s offer, addressed Dog's initial comment. "Fox has made me realize how essential it is to hear everyone's views. I'll be sharing a lot more of the responsibility around here going forward," he said.

"That's great," Dog said. "Employees are happier when they are engaged."

Fox smiled. "Okay, so there are four key issues on the board that we all agree are important to this business. Do any of these issues have obvious solutions?"

"I think that the bank covenant issue might have one obvious solution," said Owl. "Any way you look at it, the covenant is too tight. I think that I need to go back to Rat at the bank and tell him that we need some temporary relief on our covenants while we do some rethinking. I think he would be amenable to both covenant relief and perhaps temporarily increasing our line to upgrade our technology if we had a solid strategy in place to bring more of our existing content online."

"That's a great suggestion," Hedgehog said. "I think that we all have to admit that, no matter what direction we take things, the world is moving online. Even if we only use the Web to direct creatures to the ink version of the paper, we need to increase our online presence. You can count on my support. Does anyone have an issue with Owl negotiating with the bank to get some relief?"

"I like the idea a lot," Toad Jr. said. "Owl, I can help you draft a business case that shows how we can easily bring some more content online without overwhelming Rabbit's team. Coyote, perhaps we can work together to see exactly what the IT costs will be."

"My uncle was the founder of Microtus," said Fieldmouse. "I can see if I can get us some discounts on software if we go with their cloud solution."

"I think that the board of directors can also be helpful in persuading the bank to play nicely with us. Several directors are bank clients and Rat will want to be on their good side," Hedgehog said.

"Our family runs our personal trust business through the bank," said Toad Jr. "I'll ask Father to talk to Rat as well. Dad and Rat's father play bridge at the club. Perhaps he can be an influence, too."

"I'd appreciate that, Toad Jr.," Hedgehog said.

"This is fantastic," said Fox. "The covenants were a huge problem because no matter what we wanted to do, they prevented us from doing it. Owl, if you can get relief, that would be great."

"It's not guaranteed," said Owl, "but I think if we explain that we don't want relief because it's business as usual, but we want relief to try something new, we might get some flexibility. In fact, I know you'd like me in this meeting, but I want to call Rat and have an off-the-record conversation with him about this."

"Good idea," said Hedgehog as Owl excused herself from the table.

"Okay, Fox said. "So the issues now look like this:"

| Identify (Gather) Anticipate(Generate) | Clarify (Evaluate) | Set Priority (Agree) | | |
|---|---|---|---|---|
| | | Can | Must | Pri |
| Top ad clients asking for permanent discounts | Raccoon, Bear, Turtle, Magpie (top 20 percent of ad revenue) want 15 percent discount ($225,000) | Y | Y | H Hhog Squrl Owl TJ |
| Paper irrelevant | Only 30 percent of Toad Hollow residents read paper daily | Y | Y | H Rabbit Deer |
| *Gazette* lacks identity. | What are we? What is our role in Toad Hollow? In world? | Y | Y | H Hhog Board |

Fox continued. "Advertisers want cheaper rates, you don't have enough readers, and you lack identity. Can you solve any of these problems right now?"

Rabbit spoke up. "While I disagree that the paper is irrelevant, I do agree that we should be aiming to increase our readership. A number of our competitors are facing falling readership numbers just as we are, but the specialty papers are growing, as are hyper-local papers. Perhaps Deer and I can dig into who our current readers are and what they want from the paper."

"So you need time to do more research?" Fox clarified.

"Yes," Rabbit confirmed. Hedgehog wondered if that meant Rabbit planned to stay at *The Gazette*.

"What about the third issue?" Fox asked. "Can we begin to solve the issue of what identity *The Gazette* wants to have?"

"Not now," Hedgehog said. "I think it's key that the board be involved, as well as everyone around this table. Some of what Rabbit and Deer discover about our current readers will be helpful. In fact, since we are involving more creatures in the process, perhaps we should involve our readers in helping us decide who we are."

"I love it," said Toad Jr. "That's one of the ways we can use the Internet. When I launched that energy drink startup a few years ago, we crowd-sourced the product name using social media. By the time the thing hit the stores, creatures were really excited about it!"

"It sounds like two of these issues need project committees established, but we can't solve things right now," Fox summarized. "But what about the first point: Raccoon, Bear, Turtle, and Magpie, who represent 20 percent of your ad revenue, want a permanent 15 percent discount. Losing their business will cost you a lot more. Do we have all of the information needed to solve this?"

"If we don't present them with a solution today, I'm afraid they will walk," Squirrel said. "They used to do billboard advertising with Raven Outdoor Media, but last year they pulled all of their business."

"I didn't know that," Hedgehog said.

"I wanted to know if they were bluffing, so I made a call on our break. Apparently, they are serious," Squirrel said.

"New information will change the thinking process," said Fox. "That's why we like to use a method that is somewhat flexible."

"I think that we need to deal with this now," said Hedgehog.

"I agree," said Squirrel.

"Me too," said Toad Jr.

The other animals around the table were nodding their heads in agreement.

"Let's recap the process," Fox said.

## Situation Assessment Process

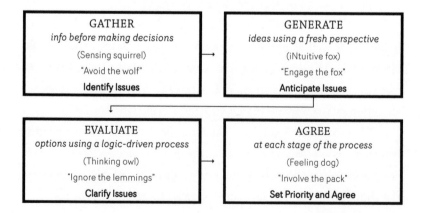

"Alrighty," said Fox. "By doing a situation assessment through identifying and anticipating issues, evaluating those issues, and seeking agreement around priority, you have clearly identified a problem that needs solving: The top 20 percent of your ad clients want a discount that will seriously compromise the bottom line of the newspaper. Let's take a quick break to stretch and grab a glass of water. Then I will show you how to start to find a solution to your problem using critical thinking."

CHAPTER TWELVE

# PROBLEM SOLVING: WHY IS THIS HAPPENING?

"So now that we have used situation assessment to determine that the key issue facing the paper is that the top four advertisers are demanding a 15 percent discount or they will pull their business, we have to figure out why that problem is occurring," Fox said. "That brings us to the problem-solving stage of the critical thinking process. Once we have identified an issue, the natural inclination is to find a solution. The trouble is that, if we don't take time to discover the underlying cause of the problem, we can rush off in the wrong direction."

He showed them the Critical Thinking Skills diagram:

## Critical Thinking Skills

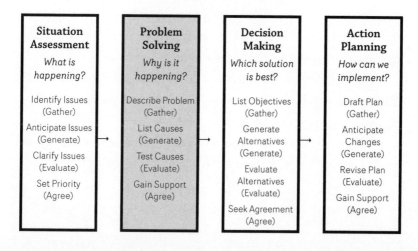

| Situation Assessment | Problem Solving | Decision Making | Action Planning |
|---|---|---|---|
| *What is happening?* | *Why is it happening?* | *Which solution is best?* | *How can we implement?* |
| Identify Issues (Gather) | Describe Problem (Gather) | List Objectives (Gather) | Draft Plan (Gather) |
| Anticipate Issues (Generate) | List Causes (Generate) | Generate Alternatives (Generate) | Anticipate Changes (Generate) |
| Clarify Issues (Evaluate) | Test Causes (Evaluate) | Evaluate Alternatives (Evaluate) | Revise Plan (Evaluate) |
| Set Priority (Agree) | Gain Support (Agree) | Seek Agreement (Agree) | Gain Support (Agree) |

Squirrel raised a paw. "But the problem here is clear," he said. "Our top four customers want a 15 percent discount on their ad rates. It does not really matter why. We can say, yes, no, or give them a counter offer. End of story."

Fox smiled. "I don't mean to pry, but did I see you take a pill with your water?"

Squirrel said. "Yes, I usually get a headache in the late after-noon."

"And what do you do to fix the headache?" Fox asked.

"I take a pain reliever," Squirrel said.

"That's what you do to dull the symptoms of a headache," Fox said. "What do you do to address the cause of the headache?"

"I don't do anything. It's just a headache," said Squirrel.

"What might be causing the headache?" Fox asked.

Squirrel shrugged.

"Does anyone know what might be causing Squirrel's headache?" Fox asked.

"He might be low on caffeine," Fieldmouse volunteered.

"He might," said Fox. "Any other ideas?"

"He might be dehydrated or maybe he did not get enough lunch," Owl said.

"His tablet might be bothering his eyes," said Toad Jr. "Maybe he needs glasses."

"Okay," said Fox, "Those are some good ideas. So if Squirrel wanted to make his headaches go away, rather than simply treating the symptoms, what would he have to do?"

"Figure out what the cause is, and eliminate it. Eat more lunch; drink more water; drink more, or less, coffee; or get some reading glasses," suggested Fieldmouse.

"When we don't know the root cause of something, it can be hard to deliver the right solution. What we know is that the top four ad clients have asked for a 15 percent discount on their ad rates. Do we know why?" Fox asked.

"Because the Internet offers a cheaper alternative," said Toad Jr.

"Do we know that, or, like the wolf, are we simply making assumptions?" asked Fox.

Toad Jr. shrugged his shoulders.

Fox projected a new image:

## Problem Solving Process

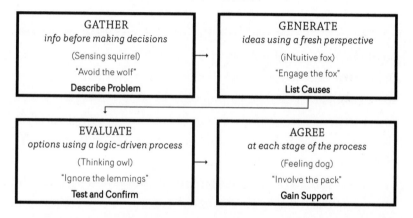

"Okay," Fox said. "Let's go back to the Great Geese Eat Apples basic thinking process. The first step is that we gather the information we need to describe the problem in as much detail as possible."

"I thought we just did that," Badger said. "We know that the top 20 percent of our clients want a permanent 15 percent discount on ad rates."

"We defined our problem statement and that's the first step, but in order to start to solve things, we need to describe the problem in more detail," Fox clarified. "Let me show you, using a problem-solving template."

Fox fiddled with his laptop and projected a new image on the overhead screen.

| Problem Statement: Raccoon, Bear, Turtle, Magpie the top 20 percent of *Gazette* advertisers—want a permanent 15 percent discount ($225,000) | | | | | |
|---|---|---|---|---|---|
| Describe symptoms | | List Causes | Test Causes | Confirm Cause | |
| | IS | IS NOT | | | |
| Who | | | | | Check Assumptions: |
| What | | | | | |
| Where | | | | | Physical Verification: |
| When | | | | | |
| True Cause | | | | | |

"Okay, so I've written down the problem statement. As Badger pointed out, that will roll out of the situation-assessment stage of the critical thinking process," Fox said. "Then, we want to gather some information about the symptoms. In other words, we want to record what evidence we have that indicates there is a problem. I find that the most helpful tool for doing this is something that I call *Is/Is Not*," said Fox.

"Wasn't Is/Is Not some band from college?" Hedgehog asked.

"I think that was Was (Not Was)," laughed Fox. "Is/Is Not is a technique used to more fully describe a problem to get to the root cause. You ask questions not only about what *is* happening, but also about what is *not* happening. For example, you might ask: Who is the animal with the problem? You then might ask, who else *could* have the problem but does *not*?"

Fox looked around the table. Everyone looked confused.

Fox continued, "In the not-for-profit example I gave you, the board asked the question, 'Who has the problem?' and learned that there were three villages in an area with similar problems with hunger and the key issue seemed to be lack of food. This led them to believe that the problem was that the area did not have enough food. Had they asked 'Who does *not* have the problem but could?' they might have discovered that there was a fourth village in the area where, even though war had the same impact, education levels were the same, and there was an agricultural economy, the creatures were not hungry. It was in an area that had been given an irrigation system by another not-for-profit organization. By asking who did *not* have the problem, my client might have looked for evidence of villages without the problem and figured out that lack of irrigation, not lack of food, was the root cause of the hunger problem."

"So we need to find out if there are any clients who are *not* asking for a decrease in their rates?" Hedgehog asked.

"Well, it would be useful to know why some clients want discounts and others don't," Fox agreed.

"I suppose," said Hedgehog.

"You can also ask: Where is the creature, object, or process with the problem? Where could the problem be happening, but is not?" Fox continued. "By asking more specific questions, you can get more specific information."

"I like that; gathering all of that specific information must appeal to the natural senser in me," Squirrel said.

Fox nodded. "Also, you can ask when the problem was first noticed. We are looking for time and date. You can ask when the problem might have been noticed but was not."

"I would not have thought to look for that without prompting." Hedgehog said. "That would be useful information."

"The intuitive foxes in the room will more naturally gravitate to asking what is not happening because it requires some creative thinking, which they love. Engaging the sensers and intuitives and asking both what *is* and what *is not* happening can help ensure you are not jumping to conclusions."

"So when we engage the foxes and involve the squirrels, we can avoid the wolf and the lemmings?" Hedgehog asked.

"Precisely!" Fox smiled. "Here is what it looks like in more detail:"

## Problem Solving Steps

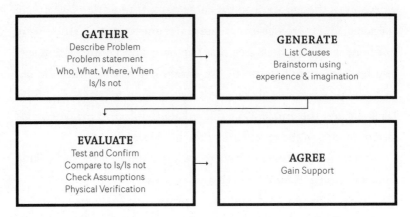

"Let's go through this together to figure out the ad rate issue. Squirrel, who is asking for discounts?"

"Raccoon, Bear, Turtle, and Magpie," Squirrel said.

"Hold on, hold on," said Fox, typing madly. "Let's start with Raccoon. Okay, who might ask for Raccoon's discount but did not?"

"What do you mean?" asked Squirrel.

"Is Raccoon your main contact on advertising issues? Does she place the ads herself?" Fox clarified.

"No, it's usually her marketing person," Squirrel said.

"Has the marketing person talked to you about the discounts?" Fox asked.

"Nope, it's all come through Raccoon," Squirrel confirmed.

"Interesting," said Fox. "Okay, did Bear contact you directly?"

"Yes," nodded Squirrel.

"And does he normally contact you to book real estate ads?" asked Fox.

"Nope, again, it's his marketing guys. Ditto for Turtle. Magpie often calls me directly but he's the only one of the four," answered Squirrel.

"Okay, good!" said Fox, scribbling.

"Now have all your clients asked for a discount?" asked Fox.

"Nope, only these guys. Mind you—they comprise the top 20 percent of advertisers, so it's no small thing," said Squirrel.

"But the other 80 percent are okay with your prices?" asked Fox.

"Well, they haven't complained to me," confirmed Squirrel.

"Alrighty. What is it specifically that Raccoon, Bear, Turtle, and Magpie have asked you for?"

"They each want a 15 percent discount on their existing ad rates going forward," Squirrel said.

"Not 14 percent or 16 percent?" asked Fox.

"Nope, each of them wants 15 percent. That's how I know they are colluding," said Squirrel.

"Have any of them asked for anything else?" asked Fox.

"Nope. They want to do the same business with us as always but want to pay 15 percent less." Squirrel said.

Coyote made a tsk-ing sound.

"Have they asked for anything else to be discounted that you are aware of?" asked Fox.

"They asked Raven to discount their outdoor billboard ads," confirmed Squirrel. "He said no, and they pulled all of their business."

"Have they done this with any other service providers?" asked Fox.

"I don't know," said Squirrel.

"I apologize for having you on the hot seat like this, but this can be a very useful exercise." Fox said. Squirrel nodded. He knew that Fox was just trying to help them out.

"What reason did they give for asking for the discount?" Fox asked.

"They all gave the same reason," said Squirrel. "They said that they could advertise online for 1/20th of the price."

"And yet they asked for only a 15 percent discount," said Fox, typing wildly. "Interesting. So, they want this discount for each ad they run going forward? Not just for certain ads?"

"Yup," Squirrel said. "All issues going forward."

"Do they advertise in every section?" asked Fox.

"Raccoon is in the automotive section and sometimes has one ad in the front section, Turtle is in the travel section with the rare front section ad, Magpie is in the life section, and Bear basically owns the real estate pages."

"What about the other sections?" Fox asked.

"News, business, and sports are basically not affected," said Squirrel.

"Have they asked for these discounts before?" asked Fox.

"Nope, first time. That's why I was surprised that they were so adamant. I might have expected the marketing guy to approach me first with an eventual escalation to the CEOs and our board. But here, the CEOs called me and, next thing I knew, Toad Sr. was involved," said Squirrel. "Basically, I was ambushed."

"Interesting," said Fox.

He asked a few more questions then projected the results on the screen:

| Problem Statement: Raccoon, Bear, Turtle, Magpie—the top 20 percent of *Gazette* advertisers—want a permanent 15 percent discount ($225,000) | | | | | |
|---|---|---|---|---|---|
| Describe symptoms | | | List Causes | Test Causes | Confirm Cause |
| | IS | IS NOT | | | |
| Who | Raccoon Bear Turtle Magpie 20 percent of clients contacted Toad | Marketing Staff 80 percent of clients contacted Squirrel | | | Check Assumptions: |
| What | 15 percent discount | > 15 percent or < 15 percent | | | Physical Verification: |
| | Discount | More value for $ | | | |
| | Outdoor media discount | Just *Gazette* | | | |
| Where | Every issue | Some issues | | | |
| | Auto, RE, Life, Travel | News, Business, Sports | | | |
| When | Now | Contract renewal | | | |
| True Cause | | | | | |

"So, here are the symptoms that indicate our problem. What do they tell you about what might be going on?" Fox asked.

The animals sat quietly and Fox gave them a few minutes to think. Coyote raised a paw.

"Yes, Coyote, please go ahead," said Fox.

"Well," Coyote said, "I had thought the problem would be that online advertising is killing newspapers. And maybe it is. But this particular request looks like four good old boys and girls who decided over golf to lower their costs by banding together."

"Interesting," Fox said. "Has going through this Is/Is Not exercise changed anyone else's views on the problem?"

"Why should we let a handful of customers change our business model? Talk about the tail wagging the dog—no disrespect, of course," Coyote said, shooting a look Dog's way.

"None taken," said Dog. "I agree. It's crazy to think that we are doomed. Can't we grow the sections of the paper where these guys don't play?"

Fox smiled. "This is excellent. Let's start capturing some of this on the problem solving sheet." He began typing again.

"So what do we think the true cause of the problem is?" he asked. "Is it that *The Gazette* is losing business to online advertisers, like we first thought?"

"The problem is that our top four ad clients are acting collectively to negotiate a 15 percent discount. Full stop," Hedgehog said. "It's not that all the other stuff is not a problem over the longer term, but for this problem all of those other issues were misleading us. We don't need to reinvent our business today. We need covenant relief and then a strategy to deal with these four critters."

"Does everyone agree?" asked Fox.

The animals around the table nodded.

"How do we know this is the right cause?" Toad Jr. asked.

"Great question," Fox replied. "Let's go back to that not-for-profit example. They knew that the three villages they were focusing on had problems with hunger, which they thought was caused by an inability to grow enough food. Had they found out that a village nearby grew food successfully, their true cause assumption might have been challenged. By looking at the villages that grew food, they would have seen that they had mastered irrigation. Lack of food answered the Is question but did not answer the Is Not question. Had they tested the assumed root cause against the Is Not symptoms, they might not have wasted months gathering up food that made the problem worse

| **Problem Statement:** Raccoon, Bear, Turtle, Magpie—the top 20 percent of *Gazette* advertisers—want a permanent 15 percent discount ($225,000) | | | | | |
|---|---|---|---|---|---|
| Describe symptoms | | | List Causes | Test Causes | Confirm Cause |
| | IS | IS NOT | | | |
| Who | Raccoon Bear Turtle Magpie | Marketing Marketing Marketing Others | This is a CEO/ owner driven initiative | Only CEO level involvement | Check Assumptions: Rechecked with Squirrel who confirmed |
| | 20 percent of clients | 80 percent of clients | These four seem to be colluding | No other clients have asked for discount | |
| What | 15 percent discount | > 15 percent or <15 percent | They all have the same discount request | Raccoon does more volume but has not asked for more | |
| | Discount | More value for $ | They all want money off | There is more they could ask for (more space for same money) | Physical Verification: |
| | Outdoor media discount | Just *Gazette* | They are asking all media for a break | If it were a *Gazette* problem, they'd only target paper | Talk to Toad Sr. |
| Where | Every issue | Some issues | Want the ad break always | Don't just want it to help with year end | |
| | Auto, RE, Life, Travel | News, Business, Sports | No plans to expand reach | If problem were readers, might play with placement | |
| When | Now | Contract renewal | This is not linked to a change for us | No problem in past when we lost so many readers | |
| True Cause | Same discounts indicate collusion among the four advertisers rather than a systemic issue fits all of the symptoms. | | | | |

over the long term and instead would have raised money for an irrigation system."

Hedgehog sat forward, "So comparing the true cause to the Is and Is Not statements allows you to hit the pause button before you head over the cliff with all the other lemmings," he said.

"Precisely," said Fox and pointed to the white board. "Okay, so does the collusion idea explain why the CEOs were originating the calls rather than the marketing department?" he asked.

Everyone nodded.

"Does it explain why 20 percent of the business is affected but not the remaining 80 percent?" Fox asked.

Again, everyone nodded.

"Does it explain why everyone's request was the same? Does it explain the outdoor advertising information? Does it explain why the same reason was given?" Fox asked.

All heads continued to nod.

"Does it explain the timing?" Fox asked.

"Of course," Hedgehog said. "I think we have our answer."

"Does everyone agree that this is our answer—that this ad price decrease request is simply four clients who golf together trying to reduce their ad costs?"

Nobody disagreed.

"The nice thing about involving everyone in this problem-solving process is that we can all come to the same conclusions together. What if Hedgehog had simply dismissed this as collusion right up front?" Fox asked.

"He'd have been right," observed Deer.

"True, but would you have believed him?" Fox asked.

"No," said Coyote.

"Remember," said Fox. "It is not enough to have the right answer; you must convince others that you have the right answer. What else do you need?"

"You also need buy-in," Hedgehog said.

"Right. It's all well and good to know that you have found the root cause to a problem. But if the creatures whose help you will need to solve the problem and take action do not believe that you are solving the right problem, your efforts will fail," Fox said.

"Involve the pack!" exclaimed Dog.

"Exactly!" Fox said. "Everyone needs to be involved in gaining buy-in, but creatures like you with a preference for feeling will not sign off on an idea—even if it looks 'right'—until they think everyone has bought in."

Fox poured himself a glass of ice water from the jug in the middle of the table. He took a sip. "So does everyone buy into this?" he asked, projecting the problem solving sheet.

Everyone around the table nodded.

"So that's problem solving," Fox said. "Once we have identified a problem and everyone is in agreement that we have found the true cause, what do we need to do?"

"Decide what to do about it?" Rabbit asked.

"Absolutely!" smiled Fox.

| Problem Statement: Raccoon, Bear, Turtle, Magpie—the top 20 percent of *Gazette* advertisers—want a permanent 15 percent discount ($225,000) | | | | | |
|---|---|---|---|---|---|
| Describe symptoms | | | List Causes | Test Causes | Con firm Cause |
| | IS | IS NOT | | | |
| Who | Raccoon Bear Turtle Magpie | Marketing Marketing Marketing Others | This is a CEO/ owner driven initiative | Only CEO level involvement | Check Assumptions: rechecked with Squirrel who confirmed |
| | 20 percent of clients | 80 percent of clients | These four seem to be colluding | No other clients have asked for discount | |
| What | 15 percent discount | > 15 percent or <15 percent | They all have the same discount request | Raccoon does more volume but has not asked for more | Physical Verification:

The idea that the discounts indicate collusion among the four advertisers rather than a systemic issue fits all of the symptoms. |
| | Discount | More value for $ | They all want money off | There is more they could ask for (more space for same money.) | |
| | Outdoor media discount | Just *Gazette* | They are asking all media for a break | If it were a *Gazette* problem, they'd only target paper | |
| Where | Every issue | Some issues | Want the ad break always | Don't just want it to help with year end | |
| | Auto, RE, Life, Travel | News, Business, Sports | No plans to expand reach | If problem were readers, might play with placement | |
| When | Now | Past or future | This is not linked to a change for us | No problem in past when we lost so many readers | |
| True Cause | Top four advertisers are working collectively to negotiate a 15 percent discount ($225,000) by threatening to cancel $1,500,000 in advertising revenue. | | | | |

CHAPTER THIRTEEN:

# DECISION MAKING: WHICH SOLUTION IS BEST?

"Once we know what problem we need to solve, we need to make a decision about which solution is best," said Fox, showing them the Critical Thinking Process diagram:

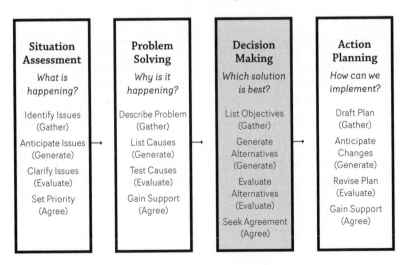

## Critical Thinking Skills

| Situation Assessment | Problem Solving | Decision Making | Action Planning |
|---|---|---|---|
| What is happening? | Why is it happening? | Which solution is best? | How can we implement? |
| Identify Issues (Gather) | Describe Problem (Gather) | List Objectives (Gather) | Draft Plan (Gather) |
| Anticipate Issues (Generate) | List Causes (Generate) | Generate Alternatives (Generate) | Anticipate Changes (Generate) |
| Clarify Issues (Evaluate) | Test Causes (Evaluate) | Evaluate Alternatives (Evaluate) | Revise Plan (Evaluate) |
| Set Priority (Agree) | Gain Support (Agree) | Seek Agreement (Agree) | Gain Support (Agree) |

"The first thing we want to do is to put on our squirrel hats and gather together a list of our objectives," Fox said. "We want to identify all of the things we want our solution to accomplish. This will help us avoid jumping to a decision too quickly, and instead make a decision that truly solves our problem. The next step is to generate some alternatives that meet the objectives. "

"Bring on the foxes," Hedgehog said.

"Indeed," agreed Fox. "The more ideas, the better. Then you need to evaluate the alternatives objectively. This is where it is important to be like an owl and avoid those lemmings that will have you jump to a solution prematurely. Having a process allows you to think critically about the proposed ideas. Finally, at each stage, we want to involve that pack so that everyone agrees. I've captured this stage in a slide":

### Decision Making Process

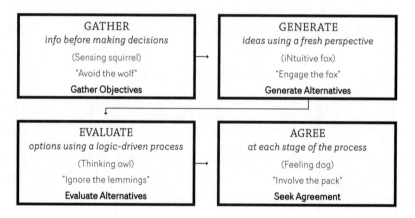

"Has everyone here read *Alice in Wonderland*?"

All the animals nodded their heads.

"Do you remember when Alice was trying to find her way out of Wonderland and ran into the Cheshire Cat? Alice asks the cat if he will tell her which way she should go. Does anyone remember what Cat replied?" Fox asked.

Coyote raised his paw. "It's my son's favorite story right now. Cat asks her where she wants to go," he said.

"That's right," said Fox. "It's a good question. If someone asks you for directions, you need to know where they wish to go. But Alice is totally lost. Her world is upside down. So she tells the Cheshire Cat that she is not sure where she is headed. And what's his response?"

"Cat replies 'Then it doesn't matter which way you go.'" Coyote said.

"Cat's point is: if you do not know where you are going, then don't be surprised where you end up. Having a view of where you want to go can be helpful in the decision-making stage of the thinking process," confirmed Fox. "Here are the key steps."

## Decision Making Steps

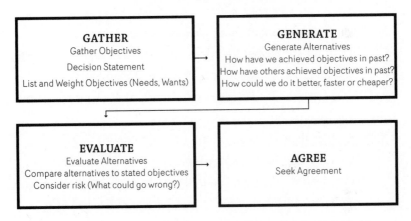

"In the decision-making process, the first thing we need to do is figure out where we want to go," Fox said, highlighting the first step:

> **GATHER**
> Gather Objectives
> Decision Statement
> List and Weight Objectives (Needs, Wants)

"This is driven off the problem statement from the last step we took," Fox continued. "A good decision statement describes the action and the end result. To go back to our not-for-profit example, let's assume that the board realized that the true problem was that certain villages did not have enough water to grow the crops they needed for food. What do they need to do in order to solve this problem?"

"Provide the villagers with water?" asked Rabbit.

"Exactly!" said Fox. "That's the decision statement. 'Supply the villagers' is the action. The end result is 'water.' That way, they can focus on results that yield that solution and not get distracted by other things. So in our case, what's the decision statement, keeping in mind that our problem statement was: Top four advertisers are working collectively to negotiate a 15 percent discount ($225,000)."

Fieldmouse raised his paw. "Decide what ad discount, if any, to offer our top four advertisers."

"What do you think of that?" Fox asked the group.

"I like it. It's simple but describes what we need to do," said Toad Jr. "Plus, it makes us consider not offering a discount."

"I'd like to tweak it a little to decide what ad discount or promotion, if any, to offer our top four advertisers. This keeps our mind on offerings other than a straight discount," said Rabbit.

"I love it!" said Fox. The animals around the table nodded.

"Do we need to put anything in there about deciding our online strategy? Or deciding if we need to trim back staff?" asked Fox.

"Only if it's needed to answer the decision statement question," said Hedgehog.

"Exactly! Let's capture this on paper in a decision making worksheet," said Fox.

| Decision Statement | Decide what ad discount or promotion, if any, to offer our top four advertisers | | | | | | | |
|---|---|---|---|---|---|---|---|---|
| Set objectives | Generate and Evaluate Alternatives | | | | | | | |
| | | | | | | | | |
| MUSTS | | | | | | | | |
| WANTS | | | | | | | | |

"Once you have a clear decision statement, you need to gather a list of objectives," said Fox. "We need criteria we can use to evaluate some of the alternative solutions we generate. Remember our not-for-profit example? If the board members simply stated that they wanted to buy an irrigation system, they might buy one that does not meet the needs of their clients. The system might be too expensive, or require a water source unavailable in the village. By gathering up some information in advance about what they *need* the system to do and what, in an ideal circumstance, they *want* the system to do, the board can come up with better potential solutions. Similarly, you need to decide what it is that you want to accomplish and what it is that you need to accomplish."

"Do they really differ?" asked Toad Jr.

"How many of you are parents of teenagers?" Fox asked.

Some of the animals around the table raised their paws.

"How many of you have had a conversation with your teens about needs and wants?" Fox asked.

Dog nodded her head.

"Dog, what's the difference between a need and a want?" Fox asked.

"Well, the way I explain it to my teenage daughter is that a need is something that is critically important to one's well-being: food, shelter, school, basic transportation, a couple of pairs of jeans and some other basic clothes. A want is Maggie Muskrat jeans and a data plan for a cell phone."

Hedgehog and Rabbit chuckled. They had teenagers too.

"Perfect," Fox said. "So needs are critically important and wants are highly desirable but not key to survival. There are certain things that a solution needs to accomplish," Fox continued. "In the case of our not-for-profit, they need some sort of way to bring water to the three villages. That's a must. They might also need a system that costs less than a certain dollar amount, since they have only so much funding available. Any solution that does not meet the 'must' objectives is rejected. Musts are deal breakers and cannot be ignored. Then, there is a whole list of wants. Perhaps they want the system to be manufactured locally or they want a system that can be operated with minimal training. Those wants can be ranked and assigned weights so that it is clear during the evaluation process what systems will best meet their objectives. Does that make sense?"

Everybody nodded.

"I really need you to come over to my house and talk to my daughter," said Dog.

Fox chuckled. "Our gatherers are going to be useful here as we pull together a list of everything we'd like our solution to address. And the more people you have in the room for this, the better. The process can break down if you classify something as a want that someone else thinks is a need. If anything is in doubt, we might want to call in some more stakeholders," Fox cautioned. "When setting objectives, we need to think about the three Rs: results, resources, and restraints."

He quickly scribbled on the whiteboard:

| | | |
|---|---|---|
| | Financial | ROI, cost savings, payback |
| | Operational | New processes and procedures |
| Results | Technological | New technology, methods, equipment |
| | Cultural | New norms and behaviours |
| | Strategic | New products, customers, and direction |
| | Cost | Funds available |
| Resources | Staffing | Skill requirements; resource availability |
| | Other | Materials, equipment, facilities |
| | | Physical or technical constraints |
| | | Legal, ethical, or moral considerations |
| Restraints | | Organizational values, policies, and procedures |
| | | Specific customer restraints |

"Okay," said Fox. "What we want to do is to focus on the results we want to achieve, the resources we need to use or conserve, and the restraints or limitations to be observed. Any questions?"

A number of the animals were shaking their heads. A few were taking detailed notes.

"What results do we want our solution to have?" he asked the group.

Deer stuck up a hoof. "Since the current scenario—giving the 15 percent discount—will cause a $225,000 loss in revenue, I'd say our ideal solution should cost us $225,000 or less."

"Is that a must or a want?" Fox asked.

Just then, Owl walked back into the room after her conversation with Rat at the bank.

"Owl, we were just setting some objectives that our solution needs to meet," Fox explained. "What has been proposed is this: Since the current scenario—giving the 15 percent discount—will cause a $225,000 loss in revenue, I'd say our ideal solution should cost us $225,000 or less."

"I think my conversation with Rat may change that," Owl said. "Rat is open to giving us some relief on our loan agreement. He'll grant us an extra million dollars in room if, and only if, it is part of a clear growth strategy. In other words, costs can go up by $1,000,000 but only if it's to fund growth. He made it very clear that the bank will not change our agreement to permit advertiser discounts."

"Did Rat forbid discounts?" asked Squirrel.

"Rat said that we were free to discount as long as we can stay within our current agreement, but there would be no additional room provided for straight discounting." Owl confirmed. "Currently, we have $250,000 in wiggle room."

"Don't we need that room for contingencies?" Hedgehog asked.

"We have contracts for our paper prices for the next 6 months, so I don't anticipate an increase in expenses there. As long as revenue does not slide, we can free up some of that room to give discounts to secure our advertising relationships."

"Okay," said Fox, "How does this change things?"

"Our objectives change," said Badger. "We need a growth solution that costs a maximum of $1,000,000. "

"I disagree," said Coyote. "The four clients are pressing us for an immediate discount. I think that it's bad enough that we have to consider allocating the $250,000 in wiggle room to address their needs. We should not let them influence what we do with the $1,000,000 too."

"I agree that we should just focus on the discount for now," said Fieldmouse. "We've been asked for a discount, not for an entire new growth strategy by the end of the day. To figure out what to do with the $1,000,000 and set a strategy for growth, we need to talk to more stakeholders. We need the board to be involved. Perhaps we should involve the advertisers too, and our readers. I just don't think it's the kind of thing that a group of animals—even senior executives—should decide quickly and in isolation."

"One of the toughest decisions of managers is to be able to determine what things they can decide right away and what decisions require discussion," Fox said. "Generally speaking, the greater the impact of a decision, the more time and more involvement required. I think that you are smart to shelve the strategic issues today and to focus on the tactical issue of the discount. But obviously, it's up to you."

"I don't feel prepared to decide our overall strategy right now," said Hedgehog. "I'd like to do more research."

"Alrighty," said Fox, "if everyone is in agreement, we can amend the objectives to reflect a $250,000 maximum cost."

"Are we saying that a maximum cost of $250,000 is a need or a want?" Fox asked.

"It's a need," said Owl. "We can't breach our covenants and the bank has made it clear they will not renegotiate our deal to accommodate discounts."

"Okay," said Fox. "Are there any other needs?"

"We need to not lose these four clients," said Squirrel. "They are expecting some sort of discount. If we don't give them the discount they want, we had better take them to Hawaii or something."

"We're not paying to send everyone to Hawaii," said Rabbit. "It's not a need. We could lose these four as long as we replace them with other clients."

"If we lose these four clients, my father will shut down the paper," Toad Jr. said.

The animals all turned to look at him. "Is this true, Hedgehog?" Rabbit asked.

Hedgehog nodded his head. "Toad Sr. is tired of what he sees as throwing good money after bad. If he sees a scenario with clients walking away or us having to give away all of our profits in the form of discounts to keep them, he has said he'd consider closing us down. I'd have to say it's a need."

"I'm just going to throw out a word of caution here," said Fox. "Remember, loss aversion is a very powerful thinking trap. We hate the thought of losing. Research tells us that we hate to lose at least twice as much as we like to win. If you are focused on the fact that you could lose the paper, you might not be as creative as you need to be."

"Let's clarify something," said Fieldmouse. "If we lose any of the four advertisers, will Toad Sr. close the paper for certain? Is this a must-have or a heavily weighted want? What if we lost four print clients but could replace the print revenue with online revenue? Would that be okay?"

"Dad would be fine with that," said Toad Jr. "He wants to keep the paper. It's our family's legacy. But there is a practicality too. We can't keep bleeding money. If we can bring in other revenue streams and continue as a newspaper, that would be ideal."

"Sounds like it's a high-priority need," Fox said. "Remember, there are no right answers here. The best-case scenario is carefully considered answers with maximum buy-in. Any other needs or wants?"

"The solution should maintain our current client base," said Coyote. "There is no point in offering a discount and losing the business anyway."

"I'd like a discount rate that we do not have to pass on to all of our clients," said Hedgehog. If we give a blanket 15 percent discount, I think Toad Sr. will shut down the paper. "There have to be some sort of parameters about who qualifies for the discount."

"Who should qualify?" asked Fox.

"Well," Hedgehog said, "most businesses reward their best clients—the guys doing the highest volume."

"Fair enough," Fox said, typing.

"I'd like a solution that improves our relationships with our top clients," said Squirrel, "and maybe encourages other clients to do more volume."

"I'd like a solution that does not devalue us as a brand," said Rabbit. "Doesn't discounting imply that we are not worth as much?"

"Anything else?" asked Fox.

"It would be great if the solution had an online component. The bank is pushing for it," said Owl.

"Anything else?" Fox asked.

Nobody had anything else to add.

| Musts |
| --- |
| Maximum cost of $250,000. |
| Not a 15 percent discount |

| Wants |
| --- |
| Maintains current clients |
| Rewards high-value clients |
| Improves relationship with clients |
| Does not devalue Gazette as a brand |
| Has an online component |

"Over the long term, there are lots of things to consider, but in order to come up with a response to the problem at hand by the end of the day, that seems to capture everything," Hedgehog said.

"Everyone okay?" Fox asked. Everyone nodded in agreement.

"Remember, involving the pack and seeking agreement does not mean that everyone has to be ecstatic about any given decision. It simply means that everyone had a chance to air their views, has had a chance to see the other side, and can buy into the idea even if it is not their first choice," Fox reminded the group. "Now, I'd like you to think about what weight you'd like to give to each of the wants. Let's take the next 15 minutes or so to try to assign a number between 1 and 10 to each objective to determine their relative importance."

The animals all began to talk at once. After about five minutes, Fox let out a loud whistle. The room became quiet. "Let me guess. Everyone thinks their own suggestion should be weighted a 10," he said

"Yes," sighed Hedgehog, "we will never reach consensus."

"All right," said Fox. "Let me try to help. Who thinks keeping all four clients is most important?"

"If we lose the four clients, we have a crisis on our hands in the short term," said Owl. "That gets my vote."

"Okay," said Fox. "Does anyone else agree that this is the most important short-term want?"

Everyone nodded.

"I'll assign it a weighting of 10," said Fox. "What's next most important?"

"I want a system that rewards high-value clients," said Squirrel. "That gives them incentive to increase their ad spend with us."

Everyone else agreed.

"What weighting should that have?" Fox asked. "It's a relative thing. How much less important is this step than keeping all four clients?"

"If keeping all four clients is a 10, then I'd say rewarding high-value clients is worth an 8," Fieldmouse said. Everyone nodded.

The animals worked through assigning weights to the rest of the want items, and Fox created a decision making worksheet.

| | Decision Statement | Decide what ad discount or promotion, if any, to offer our top four advertisers | | | | | | |
|---|---|---|---|---|---|---|---|---|
| | Set objectives | Generate and Evaluate Alternatives | | | | | | |
| | | | | | | | | |
| | MUSTS | | | | | | | |
| | Max cost of $250,000 Not a 15 percent discount | | | | | | | |
| | WANTS | | | | | | | |
| 10 | Maintains current clients | | | | | | | |
| 8 | Rewards high-value clients | | | | | | | |
| 7 | Improves relationship with clients | | | | | | | |
| 5 | Does not devalue *Gazette* as brand | | | | | | | |
| 4 | Has an online component | | | | | | | |

"Why did we not assign a weight to $250,000 cap on cost?" Deer asked. "Aren't the must-haves worth at least 10?"

"Excellent question, Deer," Fox said. "The must items are so critical to the survival of the business that they must be part of the solution. It's pass or fail. If, when we are analyzing various options, one of the solutions does not meet a must-have objective, we discard it as an option. Even if we find a solution that meets every one of our wants perfectly and then some, if it costs more than $250,000, we have to reject it or go back and reconsider our musts."

"Thanks for clarifying," said Deer.

"Okay," said Fox. "We've spent a good chunk of time gathering up and weighting  our objectives. Hopefully all of you have had a chance to get in touch with your inner squirrel. I know it was a tiring process, but it will allow us to avoid the wolf in the next stage, where we start to generate some solutions. It's easy to fall in love with an elegant solution and convince ourselves that we need to chase it. The work that we did in recording our objectives will keep us honest and on the right path. So now it's time to engage the fox and start to generate some alternatives. Is everybody ready?"

Everybody nodded.

"Okay," Fox said. "Now is the fun part, at least for me. Now we get to brainstorm the solutions that might address our decision statement and satisfy our objectives. We want at least three solutions but can go through as many as we wish. Sound good?"

The animals around the table nodded.

"Okay, a couple of things before we get started. We're going to run this as a brainstorming session. There are no bad ideas. The analysis will come in the next step. Second—the major pitfall here is avoiding that wolf. If you already know what the 'right' decision should be, you may not keep an open mind. So, I want to go around the table and find some solutions. Those of you in the room who are squirrels at heart will likely focus on solutions that come from your past experience." Fox hopped up to the white board.

"You should ask some key questions," he said, projecting a new image.

> **GENERATE**
> Generate Alternatives
> How have we achieved objectives in past?
> How have others achieved objectives in past?
> How could we do it better, faster or cheaper?

Fox continued, "The squirrels in the room will focus on the first two questions, which generate some possible solutions based on what you have experienced. The foxes in the room will tend to generate ideas using their imagination.

"This is where you can be really creative," Fox continued. "So, who wants to start?"

"Well, I guess we can split the $250,000 pro rata among all four advertisers," said Owl.

"Why are we contemplating giving the discounts to all four advertisers?" asked Fieldmouse. "I can see giving them to Raccoon and Bear, as they do so much volume. But Turtle is more of a stretch. And didn't you tell us earlier than there were lots of advertisers who do the same volume as Magpie?"

"I did," Squirrel confirmed. "And there are."

"It hardly seems fair to give Magpie a discount simply for being pushy. Maybe there should be a reward for those buying ads like the top three do," said Dog. "One of the stated objectives is to reward high-value clients. This current proposal does the opposite."

"I don't think you should reward Magpie," said Badger, thinking about how Magpie's love of gossip had contributed to his girlfriend breaking up with him.

"Are you ever going to forgive Magpie for blabbing about the engagement ring?" asked Coyote.

"Nope," stated Badger, folding his arms across his chest.

"But your new girlfriend is so much nicer than the other one. Magpie did you a favor!" Dog said.

"Don't care," said Badger.

"This brings up an important point," said Fox. "There is nothing magic about business. Business is just a bunch of animals who are working together toward a common goal. We often talk about being businesslike or professional, and somehow that seems to imply that we are able to strip all of our feelings and biases and emotions away when we go to work. But we can't. We are animals. If someone has wronged us, we will carry that bias into the workplace. Normally, if Badger said he did not like Magpie, it might taint the discussion of how he should be treated. Because we have clearly defined objectives, we can discuss Magpie more objectively. Not only would extending a discount to Magpie be galling to Badger, but, more importantly, it would be in opposition to one of your stated objectives. Rather than being an inhibiting factor, a good thinking process frees you up to more fully discuss the issues at hand. But what else do we need to remember?" Fox asked. "If we give $250,000 in discounts, won't Toad Sr. shut down the paper? Fieldmouse asked. "Good point." said Owl. "What else, other than a straight discount, can we offer?"

"Perhaps we could tell the top three advertisers that they each get a cash discount and then a credit toward free online advertising? Toad said. "I kind of love that as an option."

"So an option is to extend discounts only to top-volume advertisers?" asked Fox.

"I think so," said Owl. "That financially aligns their interest with ours. I guess we need a threshold amount. What do you think, Squirrel?"

"I'd say anything over $400,000 a year," Squirrel said. "That includes Racoon and Bear. Turtle is close."

"I think it makes sense to only deal with the top-volume guys but I'm not sure about a discount. If we offer no discount, we could use the $250,000 to add some more value to the three clients and get a head start on the growth strategy," said Fieldmouse. "You want us to look at what other companies are doing right?"

"That would be helpful," said Fox.

"When I worked at *The Capital City Post* they were also facing downward pressures on ad prices," Fieldmouse stated. "They decided to focus more on what their readers—and potential readers—wanted to read to increase the value to the readers and the advertisers. In their case, they wanted to read about education. Many *Post* readers work for the government or are politicians or lobbyists. They care deeply about education policy. So the paper started to organize education conferences. They wrote special supplements about education. They even bought one of those college entrance exam preparation companies. They became the leaders in education, so that if you were interested in the topic, even if you did not live in Capital City, you'd buy the paper."

"Wow, Fieldmouse. That's an interesting perspective," said Fox. Hedgehog was surprised. He had no idea his assistant knew so much about newspapers.

"No offense, Fieldmouse, but creatures in Toad Hollow don't care about education," Coyote said.

"But they care deeply about personal finance," Rabbit said. "After Glenwide Mortgage went bankrupt, that became the number-one concern. It's why I wanted to hire Suzy Sparrow as a money columnist."

"I think that helping our readers understand money is something good we could do. Toad Hollow was hit hard in the recession but other communities were hit hard too. If we had a focus on keeping solvent in hard times, I bet we'd get other readers if it were accessible online," Hedgehog said.

"*The Post* had great online content—podcasts and such—in addition to some special newspaper supplements. They also offered some online training seminars for teachers. They wanted to own the education space," said Fieldmouse. "Now they do, and they charge huge ad rates to people looking to reach the educated reader."

Fox thought that Hedgehog had one heck of a fantastic assistant in Fieldmouse. "Fieldmouse, have you ever considered going into consulting?" Fox asked.

Fieldmouse grinned, "After I got my MBA from Hogsford, I considered it, but I'm way too committed to playing ultimate frisbee after work and on the weekends to adopt that crazy lifestyle."

Hedgehog had no idea Fieldmouse had an MBA. He'd been his predecessor's assistant and he'd never really bothered to ask. This was a good lesson in never underestimating your teammates.

"So for a fourth option, we could use the $250,000 to put together some sort of specialized content that works with the advertiser's readership base?" Fox suggested.

"Raccoon, Bear, Turtle, and Magpie all run businesses that would have been hit hard by the recession, right?" asked Deer.

"Cars, houses, travel, and jewelry are certainly not recession-proof," Owl confirmed.

"I imagine they operate their businesses quite differently now," continued Deer.

"I've noticed that their ads have changed a lot over the last few years," Squirrel said. "Raccoon now emphasizes low financing charges, free oil changes, and good fuel economy. Bear talks about buying homes out of foreclosure and taking advantage of low mortgage rates. Turtle advertises lower-cost destinations and talks more about once-in-a-lifetime trips, such as taking a cruise to celebrate your wedding anniversary. He's also bought an interest in a campground to cater to clients who want a more affordable vacation. Magpie—not that he will necessarily be part of this—talks about emotionally charged jewelry pieces such as—sorry Badger—engagement rings. He also advertises his gold- and jewelry-buying business. He operates a quasi-pawn shop over there now."

"Those kinds of ads would be perfect for a personal finance section, would they not?" Coyote asked. "Can't we have articles that talk about the rise of those gold-buying shops or how to invest in distressed real estate? The content would showcase the ads."

"That's getting dangerously close to advertorial," said Rabbit. "We don't want to seem as if we are selling the same things our advertisers are."

"I'm not suggesting advertorial," said Coyote. "But our readers are interested in saving money. Our advertisers happen to be some of the foremost experts on doing that. At the end of the day, everyone is selling something. Turtle sells trips and writers sell their words."

"I get what you are saying and, believe me, I want to see a personal finance section. I'm just wary of any approach that could potentially devalue *The Gazette* as a brand," Rabbit said. "Not devaluing our brand is one of our stated objectives as well."

"What if the top three guys sponsored Suzy Sparrow to write a column for us and do a speakers series or something?" suggested Fieldmouse.

"I like that," said Hedgehog.

"But they want a discount. They don't want to pay *more* money," said Squirrel.

Fox interrupted, "I like how some of the back-and-forth is helping us to generate new ideas," he said. "Remember, we are still in brainstorming mode. Once we have generated all of the ideas, there will be lots of time to judge their merits based on the agreed-upon objectives. Let's ask: How have we accomplished these or similar objectives in the past? How have other organizations accomplished similar objectives? How could we do it better, faster, or cheaper than in the past?"

"I think we need to create a new ad package to get them to increase their volume. With a larger spend, you get a discounted rate, title sponsorship of the personal finance section and conference, and complimentary advertising online," said Deer.

"Advertise where online? A new section? Toad Jr.'s page?" Badger asked.

"If we do anything online, I'm going to need money to upgrade our IT systems," Coyote reminded them.

"Okay, I just want to remind you that we are solving for our agreed-upon decision statement." Fox said. "Decide what ad discount or promotion, if any, to offer our top four advertisers."

"Are we getting off course?" asked Deer.

"A little," nodded Fox. "It's a fine balance. All of these great ideas can help spark creativity. But we want to make sure we are not just generating ideas, but more specifically we are generating ideas that address the decision statement."

"I'm lost," said Dog. "What has been proposed so far?"

"That's the thing about this process," said Fox. "It can be confusing. It's why it makes sense to check in, see where we are and see if we can simplify it somehow. So far, here are my notes on what we have discussed as possible solutions and some comments." He flashed his notes on the overhead screen:

*Offer 15% discount to all 4 advertisers who asked*
- *Close to bank covenants*
- *Toad Sr. will shut down paper*
- *Eliminate?*

*Offer 15% discount to advertisers over a $400K threshold*
- *Could be close to bank covenants*
- *Toad Sr. will shut down paper*
- *Magpie will be very unhappy*
- *Eliminate?*

*Offer lower discount to all 4 advertisers who asked*
- *Not fair to others at Magpie's level*
- *Unethical to treat clients differently?*

*Offer lower discount to advertisers over $400K*
- *Worth further discussion*

*Offer no discount but another incentive (partnering opportunities, online offer?) to all four who asked*
- *Not fair to others at Magpie's purchase level*
- *Unethical to treat clients differently?*

*Offer no discount but another incentive (partnering opportunities, online offer?) to advertisers over $400K*
- *Worth further discussion*

"Do you have any comments?" Fox asked.

"I think that we can eliminate the first two options based on our covenants and the fact that Toad Sr. will shut us down," said Field-mouse. Everyone around the table agreed.

"I think that a $400,00 advertising spend threshold makes sense for any discounts or partnering opportunities," said Squirrel. "Magpie will have to up his spend. I think we can eliminate any option that invloves him out of fairness to others."

"If everyone is in agreement, then I think that we have narrowed our six options down to three." said Fox, highlighting his notes:

1. *Offer lower discount to advertisers over $400K*
2. *Offer no discount but another incentive (partnering opportunities, online offer?) to advertisers over $400K*
3. *Offer a golf trip to Bear, Racoon and Turtle to thank them for high tier business and offer no discount but another incentive (partnering opportunities, online offer) to advertisers over $400K*

Fox projected the decision making worksheet where he'd been recording their options to discuss:

| Decision Statement | Decide what ad discount or promotion, if any, to offer our top four advertisers | | |
|---|---|---|---|
| Set objectives | Generate and Evaluate Alternatives | | |
| | Offer a 15 percent discount to all 4 clients who asked ($225K) | Offer smaller discount to all clients with ad budgets >$400K. | Offer no incentive and use $250,000 to create new ad offering for >400K spend |
| MUSTS | | | |
| Max cost of $250,000 | | | |
| WANTS | | | |
| Maintains current clients | | | |
| Rewards high value clients | | | |
| Improves relationship with clients | | | |
| Does not devalue *Gazette* as brand | | | |
| Has an online component | | | |

"We know we can't afford the first option, offering the 15 percent discount, so why is it up there?" Coyote asked.

"Great question." Fox said. "If we offer the lower discount and all four creatures pull their ads, don't you think the board will want to see that we at least considered the proposal?"

"Absolutely," Coyote agreed.

"Remember, we are not only after the optimal solution to our problem, but one that the stakeholders will embrace," Fox said.

"Makes sense," said Coyote.

"So, are all of the options on the board? Anything missing?" Fox asked.

"Looks good to me," Hedgehog said. The others were nodding in agreement.

"It's time to move onto the next step," said Fox.

---

**EVALUATE**
Evaluate Alternative
Compare alternatives to stated objectives
Consider risk (What could go wrong?)

---

"What's the key pitfall to remember during the evaluation process?" Fox asked.

"Ignore the lemmings," said Rabbit. "We want to fully evaluate things—not just jump to conclusions. Is there anything we could do at this point to make sure we have all alternatives for the $250,000 on the board."

"Hedgehog, can you make a call to Toad Sr.?" asked Squirrel. "I'd bet my bottom dollar that we have to give something to the advertisers to placate them, but Toad Sr. is their friend and perhaps he'd be the better judge of that. This is his company so perhaps he ought to be involved."

"Great idea!" said Fox. "Involve all the stakeholders. Can you do that, Hedgehog?"

"Sure," Hedgehog said, trying to make his voice sound more enthusiastic than he felt. He had a feeling that Toad Sr. thought he was incompetent, and he hated to have to rely on his advice. He felt that he was paid to deliver answers, not ask questions. Mind you, Fox was paid to ask questions all the time.

"Why don't I call with you," said Toad Jr. "Might help smooth the waters."

"That's great," Hedgehog said. "I really appreciate that." Had Toad Jr. made this offer even this morning, Hedgehog would have been suspicious, thinking that Toad Jr. was trying to undermine him somehow. But now he truly felt that Toad Jr. wanted what was best for the company.

Hedgehog and Toad Jr. went to Hedgehog's office and called Toad Sr.

"Yup?" Toad Sr. answered.

"Dad, it's me. I've got Hedgehog with me on the line. We need to talk. What's that bubbling noise?" Toad Jr. asked.

"I'm in the hot tub," Toad Sr. said. "My back was sore after golf today."

Toad Sr. was always in a good mood when he was in the hot tub. Likely he was smoking a cigar and nursing a glass of gin. This was very good news, indeed. Toad Sr. gave Hedgehog the thumbs up, a trick he'd learned from the Phyllomedusa frogs—the only genus of amphibians to have opposable thumbs—when he'd spent that winter driving for a racecar test team in South America.

"You tried to play from the rodent tees again, didn't you?" Toad Jr. asked.

"I always feel like such a fool playing from the amphibians'," said Toad Sr.

Hedgehog had never heard him express any vulnerability. It was a good idea to have Toad Jr. on this call.

"What's up?" Toad Sr. asked.

Toad Jr. and Hedgehog filled Toad Sr. in on the issues they were discussing. Toad Sr. was pleased they were putting so much thought and effort into the decision. He agreed that they should not extend a discount to Magpie unless he upped his ad spend to the level of the others.

"If he wants to be a big dog, he'll have to buy his way in," Toad Sr. croaked in between puffs on his cigar.

He thought about the question they were asking him about the necessity of offering the clients a cash discount. He agreed that the 15 percent discount was out of the question. "Don't even consider the 15 percent," he said. "I own this paper. If the four clients walk, it's a signal that the business is in trouble. At that point, I'll be looking to shutter the paper and I'll deal with the board. As for smaller discounts, I'm not sure. Half that much might be acceptable—7.5 percent perhaps. Raccoon, Bear, and Turtle all sustained big losses after Glenwide failed. They are great business owners and now that they have contained their losses and have survived the worst, they are looking to take advantage of the depressed economy to push themselves ahead. I don't think that they need the discount to stay solvent. I think they want to see some immediate savings. I also think they want the ego boost of trying something on with us. I think they'd be more excited about the prospect of getting in on the ground floor of something new. They are all investors, and a bit speculative. I think they might like the idea of being partners with us in a new strategy, and the personal finance thing sounds like a fit. Everyone is excited about going online, so let's focus on that. All we discuss at the golf club are ways to safeguard our assets. I think we should offer them some other kind of incentive."

"Squirrel suggested that he take them to Hawaii," Hedgehog said.

Toad Sr. chuckled. "I like that Squirrel. He's got moxy. They've all been to Hawaii. But I bet that they'd love some great rounds of golf. We get tired of playing at the club all the time. But since we are paying a hind leg for membership, we feel guilty playing anywhere else. Tell Squirrel to buy them a couple of rounds at the best courses in the county. Maybe organize a weekend away at Pinegrove. Squirrel can be the fourth player and explain our strategy for growth over beer at the 19th hole. Spend 20 or 30 grand."

"Great," said Hedgehog. "He'll like that. Thank you so much for your input."

"Thanks, Dad," Toad Jr. said, hanging up the phone.

They walked back into the boardroom where the animals seemed to be discussing all of the options to consider. Everyone grew quiet when Hedgehog and Toad Jr. took their seats around the table.

"Toad Sr. believes that we need to offer some incentive to keep our current clients, but not necessarily cash incentives," announced Hedgehog. If we offer the 15 percent discount, he will shut down the paper. Also, he does not feel we should reward Magpie unless he ups his spend, but would like to give something to Bear, Racoon and Turtle to honor them for their loyalty through hard times."He thinks they'd like a golf weekend boondoggle costing about $25,000. And to be in on the ground floor of whatever we do in the future."

"Okay," said Fox, "it sounds like we need to add another alternative. Let me just add this into the decision making worksheet." Fox typed furiously.

"I've got to tell you, I'm not a big fan of worksheets and templates," said Toad Jr. "I just hate getting caught up in administrivia."

"I hear you," said Fox. "I used to find lists and templates confining and was very reluctant to use worksheets when I started my career. I felt that somehow they held me back creatively and that I was too smart for them. My ideas were too big to be caught on a piece of 8 ½ by 11 paper."

"Exactly!" Toad Jr. said nodding his head.

"But I've come to love templates," Fox said. "They are such useful tools for keeping your thoughts organized. They provide a paper trail of the process you followed should your decisions be questioned at some later date. Finally, business is political. There is something about putting down the details of various options on paper that discourages creatures from pushing through flawed decisions simply because they have the support of one or two key stakeholders. Process might look like it hampers creativity, but it does just the opposite: Having a structure means you can build in some space to explore wildly creative ideas. Think of it like dance steps. Do any of you watch that show where celebrities do ballroom dancing?"

"I love that show!" Badger said.

A couple of the animals chuckled under their breaths, trying to imagine their gruff production manager watching D-list celebrity animals in taffeta gliding across his television screen.

"Think of dance steps as being like templates: the fox trot, the samba. What would happen if there were no prescribed dance steps and everyone did their own thing?" Fox asked.

"There'd be a lot of broken hooves and paws," Badger said.

"Right. Whereas because both dancers know that they are doing the samba, after a while they can almost forget about the individual steps and focus on things like interpreting the music. They can be more creative because nobody is worried about crushed hooves and paws. That's what process does. I once had the pleasure of studying under a coach who was an eagle. He used to say, 'You can get mired in the muck of content or fly on the wings of process.' Not a bad thing to keep in mind."

"I'll try," Toad Jr. said, sounding less than enthusiastic.

Fox typed quickly. "First we need to look at our needs. Do all alternatives adhere to the required objective of costing less than $250,000?"

"Okay," Fox said. "So at this point, we can officially eliminate the option of offering a 15 percent discount since it does not meet Toad Sr.'s 'must' objective. We'll keep it in our notes to show that it was a consideration, but we do not have to analyze it further. Now what we need to do is to evaluate the other options by reviewing them against the objectives we generated earlier today. Let's have a quick stretch, because this is the most detailed part of the process. The thinking sensers in the room will love how elegant this decision making process is. The intuitives might find it a bit dry. But stay with me. I promise that it will be worth your while."

| WT | Decision Statement | Decide what ad discount or promotion, if any, to offer our top four advertisers. | | | |
|---|---|---|---|---|---|
| | | Generate and Evaluate Alternatives | | | |
| | Set objectives | Offer a 15 percent discount to all 4 clients who asked ($225K) | Offer a 7.5 percent discount to all clients with ad budgets >$400K. | Offer no incentive and use $250,000 to create new online ad offering for >$400K budget clients | Offer $25K golf incentive and use $225,000 to create new online ad offering for >$400K budget clients. |
| | MUSTS | | | | |
| | Max cost of $250,000 | NO | YES | YES | YES |
| | WANTS | | | | |
| 10 | Maintains current clients | | | | |
| 8 | Rewards high value clients | | | | |
| 7 | Improves relationship with clients | | | | |
| 5 | Does not devalue *Gazette* as brand | | | | |
| 4 | Has an online component | | | | |

# CHAPTER FOURTEEN

# DECISION MAKING: EVALUATING SOLUTIONS

"Does everyone see how the template organizes our thoughts?" Fox asked. "We list the alternatives being considered along the top and the objectives we determined were important down the side. The weighting of those objectives is recorded along the far left side. I've recorded those weights throughout the worksheet because we are going to use them to evaluate the solutions proposed. Does everyone see that?"

| WT | Decision Statement | Decide what ad discount or promotion, if any, to offer our top four advertisers. | | | |
|---|---|---|---|---|---|
| | | Generate and Evaluate Alternatives | | | |
| | Set objectives | Offer a 15 percent discount to all 4 clients who asked ($225K) | Offer a 7.5 percent discount to all clients with ad budgets >$400K. | Offer no incentive and use $250,000 to create new online ad offering for >$400K budget clients | Offer $25K golf incentive and use $225,000 to create new online ad offering for >$400K budget clients. |
| | MUSTS | | | | |
| | Max cost of $250,000 | NO | YES | YES | YES |
| | WANTS | | | | |
| 10 | Maintains current clients | | | | |
| 8 | Rewards high value clients | | | | |
| 7 | Improves relationship with clients | | | | |
| 5 | Does not devalue *Gazette* as brand | | | | |
| 4 | Has an online component | | | | |

Everyone around the table nodded.

"Great! The next step is to look at each alternative and rank how well it meets the stated objective on a scale of 1 to 10," Fox explained.

"Now, I'm lost," said Badger.

"Me too," said Fieldmouse. "I thought we just did that with the numbers in the chart."

"Fieldmouse understands string theory," noted Hedgehog. "If he's lost, we're all lost."

"Okay. Let's look at the first viable alternative: offer a 7.5 percent discount to all clients who spend over $400,000 per year. Forget the weights recorded on the chart for now. How well does this alternative meet the objective of maintaining current clients on a scale of one to ten?"

"I think it's a 7 or 8," said Rabbit. "I think that there is a risk someone will leave because they are not getting the 15 percent they requested. But it's less risky than offering no discount at all."

"Remember, there is no perfect answer here," said Fox. "This helps us find the best answer with the most buy-in."

Hedgehog added, "I still think that a lesser discount will disappoint these advertisers. These guys are looking for a way to increase profits over the long run."

"So what does that mean in terms of ranking these four choices out of ten?" Fox asked. "Anybody want to take a kick at it?"

Squirrel sputtered, "When it comes to the objective of maintaining our existing clients, I think that offering a 7.5 percent discount for clients above $400,000 per year ranks a 5 out of 10. True, you don't risk losing the others at Magpie's level, but I believe that Magpie will be gone for sure. He has a lot of pride, and if he is the only one out of the four to not be given a discount, he will get angry and walk. I think it is less of a slap in the face to Magpie and it has higher perceived benefit with the top three advertisers. If I ask you for $20 and you offer me $10, I feel cheated. If I ask you for $20 and you tell me that you can help me make $50, that intrigues me. I'd rather have the partnering opportunity and a shot at $50. So I rank that an 8 out of 10."

"I understand why we don't want to let Magpie in on a cash discount, but should we let Magpie get in on this option?" Field-mouse asked.

"I don't think so," said Squirrel. "I think that any partnering opportunities need to be reserved for our top clients. We need to offer a big incentive to move up into the top tier. We can offer Magpie—and all of our clients booking at his level—the opportunity to move up a tier."

"If offering a partnering opportunity and no discount ranks an 8 out of 10 in terms of maintaining current clients, what does offering them golf and a slightly less robust partnering opportunity do?" asked Fox.

"Keeping with the same analogy," said Hedgehog, "if I ask you for $20 and you give me a high school basketball ticket and a potential partnering opportunity, I feel even more delighted because even though the monetary value of the tickets is less than $20, I know that you understand that I love high school basketball. So I rank that a 9 out of 10 because my son plays. At that point, I'm less likely to pull my business right away out of respect for our relationship. But the idea of offering a $25,000 golf incentive and using $225,000 to create a new ad offer for the top 3 clients has the highest ranking of 10 out of 10 in my opinion. I'd love to know what everyone else thinks."

The management team discussed the ideas offered by Hedgehog for a few minutes and in the end, everyone was on board with the suggested ranking.

"Okay," said Fox. "I'll drop the rankings into the decision-making worksheet and show you where I'm going with this.

| WT | Decision Statement | Decide what ad discount or promotion, if any, to offer our top four advertisers. | | | | | |
|---|---|---|---|---|---|---|---|
| | Set objectives | Generate and Evaluate Alternatives | | | | | |
| | | Offer a 7.5 percent discount to top 3 clients with ad budgets >$400K. | | Offer no incentive and use $250,000 to create new online ad offering for clients > $400K | | Offer golf incentive and $200,000 to create new online ad offering for top clients | |
| | MUSTS | | | | | | |
| | Max cost of $250,000 | YES | | YES | | YES | |
| | WANTS | | | | | | |
| 10 | Maintains current clients | 10 x 5 | = 50 | 10 x 8 | = 80 | 10 x 10 | = 100 |

"To arrive at a score, we multiply the rating we give each alternative. In the case of maintaining current clients, offering a 7.5 percent discount to the top four clients above $400,000 is ranked a 5. We multiply that by the weight we gave the category: in this case you assigned it a 10. So the total is the ranking of 5 multiplied by the assigned weight of 10, for a total score of 50. Is everybody still with me here?"

"I think so," said Fieldmouse.

"I'm still confused," Hedgehog said.

| WT | Decision Statement | Decide what ad discount or promotion, if any, to offer our top four advertisers. | | | | | |
|---|---|---|---|---|---|---|---|
| | Set objectives | Generate and Evaluate Alternatives | | | | | |
| | | Offer a 7.5 percent discount to top 3 clients with ad budgets >$400K. | | Offer no incentive and use $250,000 to create new online ad offering for clients > $400K | | Offer golf incentive and use $200,000 to create new online ad offering for top clients | |
| | MUSTS | | | | | | |
| | Max cost of $250,000 | YES | | YES | | YES | |
| | WANTS | | | | | | |
| 10 | Maintains current clients | 10 x 5 | = 50 | 10 x 8 | = 80 | 10 x 10 | = 100 |
| 8 | Rewards high-value clients | 8 x | | 8 x | | 8 x | |
| 7 | Improves relationship with clients | 7 x | | 7 x | | 7 x | |
| 5 | Does not devalue *Gazette* as brand | 5 x | | 5 x | | 5 x | |
| 4 | Has an online component | 4 x | | 4 x | | 4 x | |
| Total | | | | | | | |

"In the next column over, we record how well the proposed solution of offering a discount but no incentives to all clients above the 400K threshold meets the objective of maintaining current clients. You ranked that on 8. We multiply the 8 by the weighting for the objective of 10 to get a score of 80. There is nothing magic about the number: it is your collective judgement about how well the alternative satisfies your objectives. "

"I see," said Hedgehog.

"Okay," said Fox. "Let's move down to the next objective. How well does each solution proposed address the objective of rewarding high-value clients?"

"If we give a percentage, the more a client books, the more they save," said Squirrel enthusiastically. "With the golf or an ad package offering, I'm not sure that the volume reward is as clear as with the cash discount."

"I disagree," said Toad Jr. "I think that discounts are sort of cheesy. If I were invited into a partnering opportunity, however, I'd feel really valued. But I think that Raccoon needs to be especially recognized because she does so much business with us. She does almost $75,000 more than Turtle, right? Maybe we need gold, silver, and bronze sponsors."

"That's a great idea," said Rabbit. It was shocking to hear her say anything positive about Toad Jr. "Can we change the solution a bit?"

"If everyone agrees, of course," said Fox. "Remember there are no hard-and-fast rules here. There is no right answer. We simply want to get lots of options on the table. We want to evaluate those options and we want people to buy into the best solutions. That's what makes for good business thinking."

The management team discussed all of the solutions and evaluated them against the stated objectives. Fox showed them what they'd concluded:

| WT | Decision Statement | Decide what ad discount or promotion, if any, to offer our top four advertisers. | | | | | |
|---|---|---|---|---|---|---|---|
| | | Generate and Evaluate Alternatives | | | | | |
| | Set objectives | Offer a 7.5 percent discount to top 3 clients with ad budgets >$400K | | Offer no incentive and use $250,000 to create new online ad offering for top clients | | Offer $25K golf incentive and use $225,000 to create new online ad offering for gold tier clients | |
| | MUSTS | | | | | | |
| | Max cost of $250,000 | YES | | YES | | YES | |
| | WANTS | | | | | | |
| 10 | Maintains current clients | 10 x 5 | = 50 | 10 x 8 | = 80 | 10 x 10 | = 100 |
| 8 | Rewards high-value clients | 8 x 7 | = 56 | 8 x 10 | = 80 | 8 x 8 | = 64 |
| 7 | Improves relationship with clients | 7 x 5 | =35 | 7 x 8 | = 56 | 7 x 10 | =70 |
| 5 | Does not devalue *Gazette* as brand | 5 x 6 | =30 | 5 x 10 | = 50 | 5 x 8 | =40 |
| 4 | Has an online component | 4 x 0 | = 0 | 4 x 9 | =36 | 4 x 8 | = 32 |
| Total | | | 171 | | 302 | | 306 |

"Well, if everyone is in agreement, once we have ranked all of our alternatives and multiplied them by the weight of the objectives, it's simply a matter of adding up the scores in each column, as I've done in the bottom row," Fox said. "The beautiful thing about using a worksheet like this is that if at any point in the future, your decision is questioned, you can simply pull out this worksheet and show whoever asks how you reached your conclusions. So what option wins?"

"The last two options: spending $250,000 on an alternative online ad option for the top three candidates and spending $225,000 on the same thing plus some golf are virtually tied at 302 and 306," said Owl.

"So what do we pick?" Hedgehog asked, disappointed that the answer was not clear.

"Excellent question," Fox said. He then went over to the whiteboard and wrote down four words:

| | |
|---|---|
| Radar | Kayak |
| Racecar | Raven |

"Okay, without consulting one another, I'd like you to write down which word does not belong," Fox said.

The animals read the list and recorded their answers.

"Alrighty. With a show of paws, hooves, and wings, who thinks *radar* does not belong?"

Only Dog raised a paw. "Because it's an acronym."

"Who thinks *kayak* does not belong?"

Deer, Coyote, and Badger voted against *kayak*.

"Badger, why did you choose *kayak*?" Fox asked.

"Because all of the other words start with an 'r'" he said.

"Okay, who thinks *racecar* does not belong?" he asked.

Owl, Hedgehog, Fieldmouse, and Squirrel signaled that choice.

"Why, Owl?" Fox asked.

"Because the other words are all five letters in length," she said.

"Fantastic!" said Fox. "Alrighty, Rabbit and Toad Jr., you thought that *raven* did not belong. Why?"

"The other words are all palindromes—they are the same forwards and backwards," Rabbit said. Toad Jr. nodded his head in agreement. This was the second time they'd agreed on something today.

"Clever," Fox smiled.

"So we have four solutions that have been proposed. All four are correct. So which one do we choose?" Hedgehog asked.

"Let's put it to a vote. Right now, we have one vote for *radar*, three votes for *kayak*, four votes for *racecar*, and two votes for *raven*. Would anyone else like to change their vote now that they've heard all the options?"

"I'd like to change from the *racecar* to *raven*," said Fieldmouse. "Palindromes are fun!"

"Me too," echoed Deer. "Change my vote from *kayak*."

"And, I would like to change from *radar* to *kayak*," said Dog.

"Fantastic, so we have three votes for *kayak*, three votes for *racecar* and four votes for *raven*," Fox said.

"So *raven* is the winner—or loser, as the case may be?" asked Hedgehog.

"Not yet," Fox smiled. "Is anyone going to leave the room or quit their job if *raven* is declared the winner?" Fox asked.

A few animals chuckled. "Media types are known to be temperamental," Dog said, "but I don't think anyone is going to quit their job over a palindrome!"

"Over a palindrome, no, but over other issues, they might. It's good to know if an issue is critical for any stakeholders. I'm not saying that stakeholders get to issue ultimatums to change the results of things, but it is good to know if the outcome of a decision is important to key players." Fox said. "So, at this point, I can safely declare *raven* as the word that does not belong and move on."

"So, are you saying that in the case of a virtual tie, you need to go with the solution with the most buy-in?" Badger asked.

"Precisely. If you have involved all of your stakeholders and have two or three good options on the table, chances are that any of the options could work quite well. Remember, the best solution is the best idea with the most support. If you have two best ideas, then the one with the most support will carry the day. *Raven*, *kayak*, and *racecar* are all equally correct answers, but if most creatures want *raven*, then *raven* it is," Fox confirmed.

"In that case, I say we go for the golf option," said Hedgehog. "Toad Sr. proposed it and he is the owner of the paper. But I think it's important that we considered everything so we are all on board."

"I agree," said Coyote, "if I had not been in this meeting and I heard that you were choosing to spend money on a golf boondoggle instead of moving us to the cloud, I'd have questioned your judgment. Now I know that this is part of an overall strategy to improve client relationships and build an online strategy. Presumably updated technology will be part of the execution."

"Exactly!" said Fox. "Involving others does not mean that everyone in the room gets their own way. That would be impossible. What it means is that everyone has input and understands why certain decisions were made. Execution is much less risky when there is so much buy-in."

"So the golf option is our clear winner?" Rabbit asked.

Fox shook his head. "Almost. The last step is to look at the risk associated with the two options. If the most favored option is seen as too risky, sometimes we will go with our second choice. Let's go back to our not-for-profit example. Let's say that the board has identified three good irrigation systems. What are some risks they might consider?"

Hedgehog thought a moment. "They might want to know if there is some maintenance plan available if the system breaks down. They might want to know how to keep the system secure if there is conflict in the area. They might want to know if there is a back-up plan for getting water if one of the water sources—such as a lake—is somehow compromised. Maybe one of the systems is better at collecting rain or something."

"Right!" said Fox. "They can look at what might go wrong and see what systems have the most flexibility for avoiding problems. They can also consider if there are any factors that might mitigate the risk. Having a system that can work with a backup water supply would mitigate some risk. A great option with lots of risks might be abandoned in favor of an option that meets all of the key objectives but has a lower risk of failure."

"Makes sense," said Hedgehog.

"We need to consider a few questions," Fox said. "What could go wrong? Where is our information soft or not supported by hard data? And where are we close to a must-have objective? Let's look at our two most appealing solutions: extending an online ad offering to the gold-tier clients or extending a golf vacation and a slightly less robust ad offering. What are some of the things that can go wrong? Let's brainstorm a little."

"I think in both cases, we are offering way less than the clients want. They could all decide to walk," Coyote said.

"How likely is that?" Fox asked.

"Um, low, I'd say," said Hedgehog. "From what Toad Sr. said, it's unlikely they will all pull their business. But if they did, it would be a disaster. The impact would be very high."

"And how might you mitigate that risk?" asked Fox

"Well, we need to get their buy-in to the new plan. Toad Sr. is their friend so he should be part of breaking the news to them," Squirrel said. "I think the golf plan is slightly less risky because we are offering them something tangible to show they are valued. And that might buy us the time to bring them on board as partners."

"Okay, any other risks?" Fox asked.

"Magpie could tell everyone that the top three are getting special treatment. There could be a mutiny," said Rabbit. "It's a medium probability, I'd say, and the impact is probably low. I think that everyone knows that the more you pay, the more you get."

"And how can we help mitigate this risk?" Fox asked.

"We can preempt Magpie. I can tell all of our advertisers that we are offering a new tier in case anyone wants to up their spend," said Squirrel.

"Other risks?" asked Fox.

"We are spending all of the wiggle room on our covenants," said Coyote. "That makes me nervous. There is no margin for operational error. That puts us very close to breaching the must-have objective. I think it's a slightly higher risk for the golf option since the $25,000 we spend is simply money out the door. It's a medium probability, but given how close we are to our bank limits, I think there would be a high impact."

"Owl? Any comments?" Hedgehog asked.

"It is a risk," said Owl. "But since $250,000 is being spent on moving us toward the online revenue streams that the bank is encouraging, I think the bank would support this spending."

The team talked a bit more about risk and then felt comfortable that they'd considered everything.

"When evaluating risk, we look at two things," said Fox. "We look at the probability that the risk will occur. Is there a high, medium, or low probability? We also look at the impact on the organization if the risk occurs, again using high, medium, or low. Let's take a look at what I recorded from our discussion of these two options on my risk evaluation worksheet."

"More worksheets?" Toad Jr. grimaced.

"Yes, trust me on this. This kind of structure helps you think more clearly, and helps justify your choices to others," Fox said. "On the rare occasion that things go sideways, it shows that you considered the risks and made the best decision you could with the available information. I've been teaching this for more that half my life, and it works. Take a look."

| RISK FACTORS | Offer no incentive and use $250,000 to create new online ad offering for gold-tier clients | Offer golf incentive and use $225,000 to create new online ad offering for top 3 clients |
| --- | --- | --- |
| All four advertisers will pull ads | Probability: Low<br>Impact: High<br><br>Mitigate: Toad Sr. will talk to them | Probability: Low<br>Impact: High<br><br>Mitigate: Toad Sr. will talk to them and Squirrel can talk further while golfing |
| Magpie will pull ads | Probability: High<br>Impact: Medium<br><br>Mitigate: Squirrel will offer him the same deal if he increases his business.<br>Toad Sr. will speak to him. | Probability: Low<br>Impact: High<br><br>Mitigate: Squirrel will offer him the same deal if he increases his business.<br>Toad Sr. will speak to him. |
| Magpie will tell all <$400K spend advertisers about special deal | Probability: Medium<br>Impact: Medium<br><br>Mitigate: Squirrel will call before Magpie does. Advertisers offered same deal if increase spend | Probability: Medium<br>Impact: Medium<br><br>Mitigate: Squirrel will call before Magpie does. Advertisers offered same deal if increase spend |
| No margin for operational error | Probability: Low<br>Impact: High<br><br>Mitigate:<br>Owl will talk to bank to explain that this is part of growth strategy | Probability: Low<br>Impact: High<br><br>Mitigate:<br>Owl will talk to bank to explain that this is part of growth strategy |

"Do the risk factors change your decision or do you still think that the golf incentive mixed with a good future partnering opportunity is the way to go?"

"Golf," said Hedgehog.

Everyone else at the table nodded in agreement.

"Okay," said Fox. "Well done. You have analyzed the situation, identified the problem, and found the best solution. And, because we have involved all of you, we hopefully have your buy-in. Do we?"

"Of course!!"

Fox continued: "Terrific! There is one last step in the thinking process. Luckily, it's the shortest step and then we can all go home. If I miss my plane, Mrs. Fox will make me into a winter coat. So I'm going to need everyone to pay attention."

# CHAPTER FIFTEEN

# ACTION PLANNING: HOW CAN WE IMPLEMENT?

"Once we have performed a situation assessment to figure out what is happening, problem solving to find out why it's happening, and decision making to find out which solution we should choose, we need to plan how to put that solution into action." Fox showed the team the final step in the critical thinking process.

## Critical Thinking Process

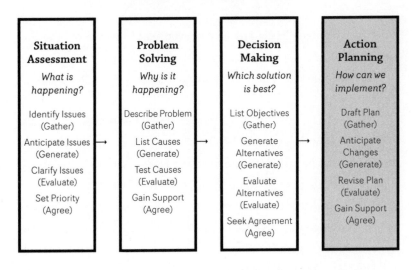

| Situation Assessment | Problem Solving | Decision Making | Action Planning |
|---|---|---|---|
| *What is happening?* | *Why is it happening?* | *Which solution is best?* | *How can we implement?* |
| Identify Issues (Gather) | Describe Problem (Gather) | List Objectives (Gather) | Draft Plan (Gather) |
| Anticipate Issues (Generate) | List Causes (Generate) | Generate Alternatives (Generate) | Anticipate Changes (Generate) |
| Clarify Issues (Evaluate) | Test Causes (Evaluate) | Evaluate Alternatives (Evaluate) | Revise Plan (Evaluate) |
| Set Priority (Agree) | Gain Support (Agree) | Seek Agreement (Agree) | Gain Support (Agree) |

"Lots of creatures can make good decisions. Where projects and businesses often fail is in the execution," said Fox. "That's why the action planning skill is so important. If you have been involving stakeholders all along, it should be fairly straightforward. If anyone is not on board, this is where you tend to find out. You need to have engaged stakeholders in order to successfully implement your plans."

## Action Planning Process

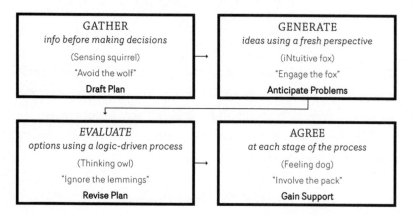

Fox explained. "Have any of you ever heard the tale of 'The Fox and the Cat?'"

"Let me guess, it's another story about how a fox is amazing," Dog chuckled.

"Not exactly," grinned Fox. "It's another one of Aesop's fables, like 'The Wolf and the Lamb.' While it's called 'The Fox and the Cat,' I think it should be called 'The Fox and the Hedgehog.' So I've adjusted it a little to reflect that. Hedgehog, you've been such a great sport today that I dedicate this final story to you. It was written a long time ago, so I apologize in advance to those of you with delicate constitutions, but here it goes."

Fox began to retell the fable:

*Once a hedgehog and a fox were traveling together. As they went along, they began to argue.*

*"You think you are extremely clever, don't you?" said the fox. "I know dozens of tricks!"*

*"Well," retorted the hedgehog, "I admit I know one trick only, but it is worth a thousand of yours!"*

*Just then, close by, they heard a hunter's horn and the yelping of a pack of hounds. In an instant, hedgehog rolled into a ball and stuck out his spines, hiding among the leaves.*

*"This is my trick," he called to the fox. "Now let me see yours."*

*The fox had so many plans for escape that he could not decide which one to try first. He dodged here and there, he doubled back on his tracks, he ran at top speed, and he jumped in and out of holes. But the hounds caught him, and soon put an end to the fox and all his tricks.*

"Gosh, what a story!" Hedgehog said.

"My mother swore that it was a true story about her great, great uncle Cedric," Fox laughed.

"Did he die?" Badger asked.

"Oh no. The hounds beat him up and then when he was recovering in the hospital he ran off with his nurse. He left the nurse for his personal trainer and then left her for the lead singer of a jazz band. He never could decide on anything and stick with it," Fox said. "And that's the whole point of action planning."

A few of the animals chuckled.

"When I first met Hedgehog," Fox continued, "I told him a quote from an ancient poet named Archilochus, who wrote that the fox knows many things, the hedgehog knows but one. I think that Hedgehog took that as a derogatory remark, but in the action-planning stage, having a leader who can take that one idea and drive it forward is critical to success."

Hedgehog smiled. He'd been feeling on edge for most of the day, as Fox had pushed him out of his comfort zone. If there was one thing he did well, however, it was executing plans flawlessly. He was glad that the process would be ending on a strong note.

"I like that story," Hedgehog said.

"I thought you might," Fox said, smiling. "It's great to know many things, but if you never do anything, it hardly matters. Sometimes we like generating ideas so much that we never move forward."

"So, now what do we do?" asked Badger.

"It's right back to Good Geese Eat Apples," said Fox. We gather, generate, evaluate, and seek agreement:"

## Action Planning Steps

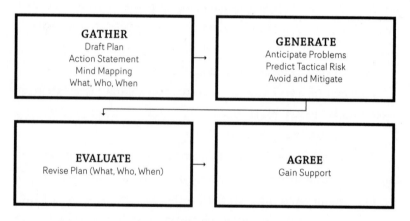

"Let's get started with the gathering stage."

**GATHER**
Draft Plan
Action Statement
Mind Mapping
What, Who, When

"The first thing we need is a simple action statement," Fox said. "We need an action, an end result, and a time frame. Who wants to take a crack at an action statement for the ad discounts?"

Fieldmouse stuck his paw in the air.

"Offer a golf perk to Raccoon, Bear, and Turtle by six o'clock today and tell them that we'd like to partner with them on an exciting growth strategy."

"Any comments?" asked Fox.

"Sounds good to me," said Badger.

"Okay," said Fox. "Now that we are clear on what we are doing, we can draft an action plan."

"What action plan?" said Toad Jr. "Squirrel has to pick up the phone. We need a plan for that?"

Fox smiled. "We might. They are expecting a 15 percent discount. Magpie is expecting to hear from us. We need to figure out what else we are going to offer them and how to get them involved. Remember the risks and what we need to do to mitigate them. Squirrel, are you okay running with this on your own?"

"I want to go over some of the steps as a group," he said. "These guys are aggressive. If I have not proactively thought through these issues, the call could blow up in my face. There is still a big risk that they are going to hate the new offer and walk."

"Okay," said Fox. "Why don't we use a technique called mind mapping to determine all the things that Squirrel should be considering before heading into this call."

Fox projected a diagram on the board:

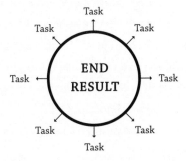

"When it comes to action planning, there is a tendency to underestimate how many steps are required to get something done. As a result, the creatures charged with implementation feel stressed if they are given more work than anticipated. Things tend to go over time and over budget. By mapping out all of the steps, everyone has a more realistic idea of what needs to take place," Fox explained. "Mind mapping is like brainstorming—we want to get the raw ideas on the whiteboard and then organize them later. The diagram I've projected shows the thinking process. Let's try to map out what needs to be done to successfully articulate a golf trip and partnering opportunity to the top three clients."

"I think that Toad Sr. needs to be involved. And the board should be on standby. We need everyone to know what we are doing," said Hedgehog.

"Perfect," said Fox. "Will you do that today?"

"I will let the board know by e-mail and follow up with Toad Sr. by phone," said Hedgehog.

"Squirrel needs to let Magpie know he won't be getting a discount unless he increases his ad spend," said Deer.

"How is that best accomplished?" Fox asked Squirrel.

"I ought to speak to Magpie in person," said Squirrel. "He's open until eight o'clock and I need to buy an anniversary gift for my wife. If I'm buying jewelry, he'll certainly be in a better mood. I'll see if he wants to increase his spend to be treated as a top-tier client. You never know. I also need to tell the top three customers about the discount. I think I should tell them by phone as soon as I've talked to Magpie. I'll push back the six o'clock deadline until nine o'clock, even though it means I will have to work until midnight to get the revised copy ready. I'll book a golf game with the three of them where we can talk strategy and arrange our boondoggle!"

"Are you going to call them individually or do a conference call?" Fox asked.

"You know, I'm not sure. They are bargaining as a group, so I would like to treat them as a group. I think that Raccoon will be upset that she's getting the same treatment as Turtle, since she buys far more than he does. I know that eventually she'll be a gold-tier client but for this call I want to emphasize that because they are negotiating as a group, they'll be treated as a group. I think that Raccoon may get annoyed and approach me separately because she'll want a better deal in respect to the online ads or the personal finance section. Treating them as a buying group may be the way to put an end to this sort of collusion," Squirrel said.

"Wow, Squirrel's thinking like a fox!" Badger laughed.

"How are you going to tell them they are not getting the 15 percent" asked Fox.

"I think I'll tell them—a conference call is making more and more sense to me—that they have all approached us for a 15 percent discount and that is simply not going to work. They are business creatures and they understand margins—they will get it. I'll tell them that as our very best clients, we want to offer them a golf trip to say thank-you for their loyalty over the years. I'll tell them that we understand that they want to see more value for their ad dollars on a go-forward basis and we want to partner with them on some new, highly confidential projects. I really do want to partner with them so that we are not spending our time working toward competing objectives," Squirrel said.

"Do you need me on that call?" Hedgehog asked.

Squirrel nodded. "I think if you are on that call, they will know that this is a decision supported by the entire company. That's why it's key to have Toad Sr. in the loop. If they don't like what we have to say, he's the first guy they will call."

"Dad's around right now," Toad Jr. said. "His Friday night poker game got cancelled."

"Anything else?" Fox asked.

"Well, I think that we should get a team in place that will drive the decision process for our next steps. I know we cannot figure out today whether we should emphasize Internet ads, special supplements that match our advertisers' businesses, or a personal finance section, but we should put a team in place and set a deadline by which they'll have made the decision," said Dog.

"I think it should be all of us," said Owl. "We should block a half-day next week to discuss this. That will give us time to do some research based on all of the things we discussed earlier this afternoon."

"The situation assessment chart we filled out earlier states who is responsible for following up with each of the issues we discussed," said Badger. "That's a good start."

"How about Monday afternoon," Hedgehog suggested. "That way we'll know how Squirrel's conversations went too."

All of the animals nodded their heads in agreement except for Rabbit, who seemed deep in thought.

"Should any other stakeholders be at that meeting?" asked Fox.

"Maybe Toad Sr. and Cardinal—he's the marketing guy on the Board of Directors—I'd like a couple of board members there," Hedgehog said.

"What about your advertisers?" asked Fox.

"I think we need to figure out our general direction first," said Hedgehog. "Otherwise, they'll be telling us the direction they want us to go—which may or may not be in our best interest."

"Okay," said Fox.

Fox projected a new image on the screen:

| Action Statement: Offer golf trip and partnering opportunity to Raccoon, Bear, and Turtle by 9:00 pm today. Tell Magpie he needs to increase spend to be eligible. | | | |
|---|---|---|---|
| Step | What | Who | When |
| 1 | Talk to Toad Sr. | Hedgehog Squirrel | Now—call |
| 2 | Advise board | Hedgehog Toad Sr. | Now—e-mail |
| 3 | Visit Magpie | Squirrel | By 7:00 pm |
| 4 | Conference call Raccoon, Bear, Turtle | Squirrel Hedgehog | By 9:00 pm |
| 5 | Set golf meeting with clients | Squirrel | Monday afternoon |
| 6 | Research issues from situation assessment worksheet | Management team | By Thursday |
| 7 | Meet to decide ad strategy | Management team, Toad Sr., Cardinal | Thursday afternoon |

"Okay, so I've simply taken the steps you identified, put them into chronological order and assigned responsibility for each one. Does everyone agree with this?" Fox asked.

"Yes," said Squirrel.

"Now that we have gathered the information about what steps you need to take, the next step is to generate some ideas about where there could be risks in the plan," Fox stated.

> **GENERATE**
> Anticipate Problems
> Predict Tactical Risk
> Avoid and Mitigate

"I thought we'd dealt with the risks earlier in the process," said Fieldmouse. "That's why we went with the solution we did."

Fox smiled. "That's an excellent point," he said. "When we looked at the risks earlier in the process, we were looking at strategic risk—the risk of our plan failing to meet our business goals. We chose the alternative that maximized our success and minimized our risk. In every plan, there is also tactical risk. There is a risk that somehow the plan will not be executed as we hoped."

"I think that the biggest risk involves the meeting with Magpie—who could get mad and pull his business—and the conference calls with Raccoon, Bear, and Turtle, who could do the same," said Toad Jr.

Fox nodded. "Those activities are on what we call the critical path. If those two steps don't go well, the plan grinds to a halt."

"So what do we do about the risk?" asked Rabbit.

"Hedgehog will help me on the conference call," said Squirrel. "Maybe he ought to accompany me on the visit to Magpie as well."

"I could do that," said Hedgehog. "I can tell Magpie that we truly value his business but can only give discounts to the top advertisers. I can tell him that lots of creatures do the same volume he does, but if he'd like to increase the volume, we'd be happy to pass on the discount to him as well. And I can buy a necklace for Cindy for when she gets back with the kids."

"Maybe, as a sweetener, we can give him a couple of trial ads on my site," Toad Jr. said. "Whenever one of the starlets gets engaged, there is always a lot of interest in what the ring looks like. Perhaps Magpie can have an ad showing a similar ring he sells. Right now that space is sitting empty. It will give Magpie some extra value and will show other potential online advertisers that we are open for business."

"I like that," said Squirrel. "Can we offer that to all of the advertisers at his level?"

"I think we can handle that. We'll need to beef up our system eventually," said Coyote.

"I think all of the options for our future ad offerings call for updating our systems," said Hedgehog.

Coyote smiled. He'd been campaigning to upgrade their systems and move to the cloud for months, but now it looked like there'd be a solid business case to support his request.

"Are there any other areas of risk we need to discuss?" asked Fox.

"This is silly and not on the critical path, but what if it rains during the golf day?" Deer asked. Deer was an avid golfer.

"Not silly at all," said Fox. "I once had a client who ran a bank. She had built a huge marketing campaign around a luxurious photo safari valued at over $50,000. Well, as the date of the draw drew closer, the political situation in the country where the safari would be taking place started to deteriorate. She feared that she might be facing a PR disaster if things did not improve, so she booked a second, equally luxurious trip to India. She talked to the travel arranger and they agreed that she could cancel either trip and incur a $2500 penalty. She figured that $2500 was a worthwhile investment if it meant saving the marketing campaign and mitigating a potential loss of $50,000 if they had to book another trip at short notice."

"That was smart," said Deer. "What happened?"

"Well," continued Fox. "The day of the draw, the Elephant/Tiger War broke out. When she called the winner, who was a business professor, he was less than thrilled to learn he and his wife would be delivered into a war zone and so she offered him the alternative trip. He was so delighted at her forethought that he wrote a letter to the president of the bank, praising them for thinking things through. The president was thrilled that they were saved from a PR nightmare and the loss of $50,000. My client was promoted to vice president the next year. Analyzing the risk and doing some forward planning can be very helpful."

"So, to Deer's point, it's worthwhile booking an alternative in case it rains," said Squirrel.

"Golf seems trivial," said Fox. "But if golf is important to your most critical client relationships running smoothly, then it's worth booking an alternative plan."

Squirrel nodded and made a few notes.

"I'm worried about that conference call," said Hedgehog. "Squirrel, I have a lot of faith in you but I'm learning to involve the pack. Do you think that Toad Sr. should be on that call?"

"Dad's pretty tight with those guys," Toad Jr. said. "It's not a bad idea to involve him as much as possible. I know he's supposed to be retired, but that paper is like another child to him. I'm sure he'd be happy to lend support."

"We should do that," Squirrel said. "The more creatures we involve, the better."

"This is good," Fox said. "You are not only doing a great job of identifying the risks—generating ideas—but are also identifying ways of mitigating those risks through some good evaluation. And you are even contemplating how to gain agreement for your plan. The Good Geese Eat Apples approach is starting to become second nature for all of you."

We've made a few changes to the plan, which is the third step in action planning:

**EVALUATE**
Revise Plan (What, Who, When)

"I've amended the action planning sheet to reflect the changes," said Fox.

| Step | What | Who | When |
|------|------|-----|------|
| Action Statement: Offer golf trip and partnering opportunity to Raccoon, Bear, and Turtle by 9:00 pm today. Tell Magpie he needs to increase spend to be eligible. | | | |
| 1 | Talk to Toad Sr. | Hedgehog Squirrel | Now—call |
| 2 | Advise Board | Hedgehog Toad Sr. | Now—e-mail |
| 3 | Visit Magpie in person | Squirrel Hedgehog | By 7:00 p.m. |
| 4 | Conference call Raccoon, Bear, Turtle | Squirrel Hedgehog Toad Sr. | By 9:00 p.m. |
| 5 | Set golf meeting with clients with rain plan | Squirrel | Monday afternoon |
| 6 | Research issues from situation assessment worksheet | Management team | By Thursday |
| 7 | Meet to decide ad strategy | Management team, Toad Sr., Cardinal | Thursday afternoon |

"Is everyone clear on what they need to do?" asked Fox.

Everyone around the table nodded.

"Then you've completed the final step of the final stage of the critical thinking process," said Fox. "You've agreed on an action plan."

"So that's it?" asked Hedgehog.

"That's it," smiled Fox. "To recap, the critical thinking process consists of four skills: situation assessment, problem solving, decision making, and action planning:"

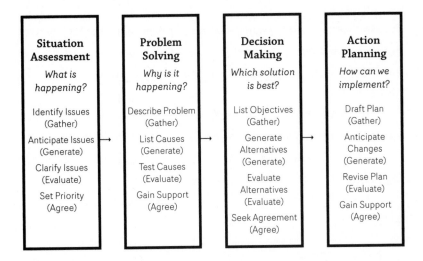

| Situation Assessment | Problem Solving | Decision Making | Action Planning |
|---|---|---|---|
| *What is happening?* | *Why is it happening?* | *Which solution is best?* | *How can we implement?* |
| Identify Issues (Gather) | Describe Problem (Gather) | List Objectives (Gather) | Draft Plan (Gather) |
| Anticipate Issues (Generate) | List Causes (Generate) | Generate Alternatives (Generate) | Anticipate Changes (Generate) |
| Clarify Issues (Evaluate) | Test Causes (Evaluate) | Evaluate Alternatives (Evaluate) | Revise Plan (Evaluate) |
| Set Priority (Agree) | Gain Support (Agree) | Seek Agreement (Agree) | Gain Support (Agree) |

"Within each thinking skill, there are four steps that follow the pattern of Gather, Generate, Evaluate, and Agree:"

"At each stage, you will need to tap into your inner squirrel, fox, owl, and dog. And avoid the wolves and the lemmings."

"I'll always find gathering information easier than generating new ideas," Squirrel said.

"Well, as I explained earlier, that makes sense. Literally. You are a squirrel and, as such, tend to be a senser. Gathering information is your natural preference. As a fox, I'm intuitive. I love to generate new ideas about things. Owl, what part of the process do you find comes most naturally?" Fox asked.

"The evaluation stage," Owl said.

"Right, because you are a natural thinker. Dog? How about you?"

"I like to try to get everyone to agree. I guess it goes along with being in AR," she said.

"It does. It's a great fit for your personality type," said Fox. "You are a natural feeler and believe the right decision is the one accepted by the most creatures. But the great thing is—and we saw it here today—we can all be good information gatherers, idea generators, idea evaluators, and agreement seekers. You've all worked really hard today. It was a pleasure to get to know all of you, but I must dash to catch my plane. Hedgehog, I'll call you in a month to find out how things went."

Fox packed up his things, walked around the table shaking each creature's paw or hoof and giving them a copy of his business card.

Before he exited the room, he held up two digits on his front right paw: "May the process be with you," he said.

# EPILOGUE

## ONE MONTH LATER

Hedgehog was sitting in his office catching up on some e-mail when his telephone rang.

"It's Mr. Fox for you," Fieldmouse said.

"Put him through," said Hedgehog.

"Hey, Hedgehog. It's Fox. I just wanted to call, as promised, and see how things were going."

"Gosh, it's good to hear from you," said Hedgehog. "Things are going well."

"How are Cindy and the hoglets?" Fox asked.

"They are really great. Cindy's physiotherapy practice is thriving. Calvin made the Toad Hollow High varsity basketball team. Bridget has the lead in her school play. Life's good!"

"Wonderful, glad to hear it," said Fox. "Say, how did everything turn out? How did the advertisers react to the discounts proposed?"

"Well, Magpie did not take it well at first. He threatened to pull his ads. But then he realized that we were offering him some good value with the trial ads on Toad Jr.'s site. Toad Jr. had exclusive photos of Maggie Muskrat's engagement ring last week, and Magpie said that his phone has been ringing off the hook from creatures who have seen his ads. He's considering moving his business online. We also offered the other advertisers at his level the same opportunity. We are not making any money from them for the next 6 months but we have had some inquiries from advertisers outside Toad Hollow who are interested in online ads. Toad Jr. is spinning off a celebrity baby blog and has one of the formula makers underwriting it. They are essentially paying for our new IT system."

"That's great news!" said Fox. "What about Raccoon, Bear, and Turtle?"

"Well, at first they were not thrilled that they were not getting a discount. But they also understood that we had no room to do so. They were thrilled that we wanted to recognize them with the golf trip. They appeared keen to know what direction the paper was taking and seemed pleased that we wanted to partner with them and valued their input."

"So how was the golf?" Fox asked.

Hedgehog chuckled: "Well, for the first outing, Squirrel was supposed to take them golfing the day of a terrible thunderstorm. There was lightning everywhere. Mayor Beaver's dam got hit."

"Oh, dear," said Fox.

"Yes, obviously that put the kibosh on the game. Luckily, Squirrel had a back-up plan in place—as you encouraged him to do—and so he asked the clients if they wanted to reschedule or go to a wine tasting at a local vineyard. They had all cleared their schedules and opted for the wine tasting—pleased at his foresight. He called me, and I joined them for the tasting, as did Toad Sr. I guess they were all feeling nice and relaxed because they were very open to what we had to say."

"And?" Fox pressed Hedgehog to continue. "What direction are you taking?"

"Well, last week Toad Sr., Squirrel, Rabbit, and I approached Toad Hollow Bank about sponsoring a personal finance section. You know they used to run lots of ads with us but they had stopped doing so. They loved the idea of a bank-sponsored personal finance section."

"Sorry to interrupt, but did you say Rabbit?" Fox asked.

"Yes," Hedgehog said. "She decided to stay. Once it became clear to her that she would have a lot of input, she was much happier. Also, she took Dog out for lunch to hear the scoop on *The Bramblethorn Banner*. Dog said that they tended to make a lot of promises they did not keep. That's why the last two editors had left within six months of being hired. Rabbit thought she was better off staying with us."

"I bet you were thrilled." Fox said.

"You know, at first I wasn't. I like Rabbit and think she's the best in the business, but I was afraid that she might be too set in her ways to work in the new *Gazette* culture," Hedgehog said.

"New culture?" Fox asked.

"I'm going to roll out your critical thinking process to everyone. In fact, I'd love to hire you to come in and do a couple of training sessions over the next few months," said Hedgehog. "I want a culture where the pack is a lot more involved. I thought that Rabbit might be too top down, but she loves the new culture a lot. She's even started to blog!"

"Seriously? That's great!" said Fox.

Hedgehog continued, "After the crash caused by the mortgage-backed securities failure, banks got a bad rap and they were all trying to deal with their reputational damage by presenting themselves as being more helpful. Toad Hollow Bank liked the idea of finance seminars, and they are sponsoring weekly columns by Suzy Sparrow to run in print and online. Then in six months, Suzy is going to appear at our first annual personal finance forum. Meanwhile, we are training a couple of our writers who have business backgrounds so that we develop additional in-house expertise. We are holding a Snoutbook contest for readers to win a financial makeover, including a check for $5,000 to help pay down their debts. The nice thing is, not only is the bank paying us for the sponsorship rights and advertising, but they have shown some flexibility around our covenants," said Hedgehog.

"That's wonderful!" said Fox. "So are Raccoon, Bear, and Turtle advertising there?"

"Well, that part of the story is a little more rocky," said Hedgehog.

"Bear saw a real estate fit with our personal finance focus. No matter the state of the economy, animals still need a burrow or a den, and he could see articles on mortgages and tips for buying an income property being helpful to his business. Raccoon thought it was a less obvious fit but could see the merit in putting in some ads for hybrids if there was an article on saving money at the gas pump. Turtle was our hardest sell. His travel business was really hurt by the recession. Animals need housing and transportation but can do without a winter cruise. He felt that the personal finance section—with its emphasis on paying down debt and delaying gratification—would hurt his business. He's taken his ad order down to Magpie's level. We are not passing the high-volume discount on to him for print advertising but he is advertising online. Maggie Muskrat got engaged in Turks and Caicos, and Turtle got a few calls about that, which made him happy."

"What did the advertising cutbacks do to your numbers?" Fox asked.

"Well, it was not great. Nobody was happy about it. Squirrel was devastated. The board went crazy. It was good that we had the decision-making process documented as well as we did because I had to justify the decisions we had made. The truth is, I think Turtle's business is really not doing well. I suspect he would have been decreasing his ad spend anyway. This allowed him to save face, saying he was decreasing his spend for strategic reasons rather than financial. But I suspect this might have happened no matter which option we chose."

"And how are things going on the financial front for you?" asked Fox.

"Well, the decrease in ad revenue hurt. Thankfully, Toad Hollow Bank stepped in with their ad commitment, which far exceeded the loss with Turtle. So on a net basis, we are slightly better off in the short term and potentially far better off in the long term. We have a new IT system paid for by Toad Jr.'s advertisers. We have a personal finance focus that excites everyone, and the bank is funding it. Our top two clients are happy, and the rest seem content for now.

Of course, I'm not going to rest on my laurels. You taught me how important it is to involve the pack, especially for a non-dog like me. I'm going to host client meetings with Squirrel once a quarter just to see what's going on. I like surprises for my birthday but not for my business."

"Hear, hear," said Fox. "Anything else going on?"

"Well, we want to look at our revenue model in general," said Hedgehog. "A lot of papers are looking at establishing paywalls for online content and trying to figure out other ways to make money for something that creatures expect to get for free. I promised the board I'd look into it and would love some coaching from you to help me devise an online revenue model. Also, I'd like to give Rabbit some management coaching. She's now dealing with young bloggers and refers to them as Generation Whine. I think she could use some help. And Fieldmouse has revealed unexpected depths. He could eventually run this new paper. As could Toad Jr. We should consider leadership training for both."

"I could help you with that too," said Fox.

"Is there anything that you can't help me with?" Hedgehog asked.

Fox smiled. "Well, Hedgehog, as I told you that very first day when I met you in the bar, the fox knows many things . . . "

# SUGGESTED READING LIST

Gladwell, Malcolm. *Blink: The Power of Thinking Without Thinking* (New York: Little, Brown, & Company, 2005)

Haidt, Jonathan. *The Happiness Hypothesis* (New York: Basic Books, 2006)

IBM Global Business Services. *Making Change Work*

Kahneman, Daniel. *Thinking, Fast and Slow* (New York: Farrar, Straus and Giroux, 2011)

O'Keeffe, Andrew. *Hardwired Humans* (Royal Exchange, Australia: Roundtable, 2011)

Dresner, Advisory Services. *Business Intelligence Marketing Study*, 2012, (www.dresneradvisory.com, *Wisdom of Crowds*)

Vroom, Victor. *Leadership and Decision Making*, 1973